£1.45

A Time For Everything

I THOUGHT when summer ended,
  I'd feel so very sad,
Because of all the outings, and the
  sunshine that we'd had.
But now the nights are cooler, and the
  leaves are falling down,
And they make a crunchy carpet of
  a lovely russet brown.
I think about my crimson curtains drawn
  against the night,
Of the fire so brightly burning, and
  the room so full of light.

The two of us in easy chairs, relaxed
  and warm, will sit.
You will read and study, and I, of
  course, will knit.
And out of deep contentment, across
  at me you'll look,
And fill my heart with gladness —
  and then resume your book.
Perhaps an endless summer might
  well begin to pall,
With thoughts like these within my
  mind, I don't feel sad at all!

Miriam Eker.

People's Friend Annual

CONTENTS

SCENIC VIEWS J. Campbell Kerr • BACK COVER Mallaig Harbour

A Box Full Of

H EATHER LENNOX gave a little gasp of annoyance as she turned the corner into Main Street. For, although she'd been only a few minutes late in leaving the office, there was her bus just drawing up to the stop. And if she missed it she would have to wait twenty minutes for the next one.

As she sprinted along, however, she saw that a familiar figure had paused with one foot on the bus platform, and was beckoning her on.

"Good old Graham Shaw!" She chuckled to herself. He was using his delaying tactics, just as he used to do years ago when she was running for the school bus.

When the dark-haired young woman finally reached the bus stop, Graham grabbed her arm and pushed her up the steps ahead of him.

"Thanks a million!" Heather managed to gasp as she fished out her season ticket.

"Yes! I can see your boyfriend looks after you," the grey-haired driver grinned, winking at the embarrassed young man.

When they had finally settled down at the rear of the bus, Graham turned to Heather.

"And talking of boyfriends, how is Barry, anyway?" he asked. "Is the romance still going strong?"

"Oh, yes." Heather smiled. "In fact that's what kept me late just now. We were discussing how we would celebrate our anniversary tomorrow evening."

"Anniversary!" Graham exclaimed. "But it's only married couples who have those."

"Rubbish!" Heather retorted. "Tomorrow Barry and I will have been going out for a whole year. And that needs celebrating."

"It certainly does in your case, Lenny." Graham chuckled, his grey eyes mischievous. "Up until now you've gone through at least half a dozen boyfriends every year!"

"Honestly!" Heather exclaimed, reddening. "You're as cheeky as ever you were, Graham Shaw! And don't call me 'Lenny'! I always hated that nickname."

"Sorry," Graham apologised, looking repentant. Then he added, "Actually I'm very glad about you and Barry. I only met him briefly at your New Year's party. But I liked what I saw of him."

"Then that makes everything all right!" Heather replied, trying to sound cuttingly sarcastic. But one look at her companion's smiling face and her voice softened. "And what about you, Graham?" she asked. "Haven't you set your sights on any poor girl yet? Or are you still fancy-free?"

"Oh, I don't seem to have time for a steady girlfriend," Graham

6

Treasures

By
Elsie
Jackson

answered with a sigh. "I'm far too busy. At the moment I'm frantically trying to raise money for my Cub Scouts. Our funds are desperately low. That's why I caught the later bus home from work tonight. I popped in for a chat with Laura Black, our local Brown Owl, to see if she had any bright ideas about fund-raising."

"And did she?" Heather asked.

"Yes," Graham replied. "She suggested we have one of those fifty-fifty sales, where you auction fairly pricey items . . ."

"I know!" Heather cut in. "And the person who donates them gets half of the sale money. I think that's a good idea. My cousin Marna's school has those occasionally, and they make quite a lot out of them."

Graham nodded, still looking rather doubtful.

"Just so long as we have enough stuff handed in," he remarked. "It's a different matter from collecting jumble."

"Well I'll certainly ask around and see if there's anyone who would like to contribute," Heather assured Graham as, the bus approaching their stop, they rose and made their way along the passageway to the exit doors.

"When will you be holding your sale?" Heather asked as they paused outside Graham's gate a few minutes later.

"On the twentieth of May. Two weeks tomorrow," Graham told her. "That's the first Saturday the hall's vacant."

H EATHER smiled to herself as she hurried up Northfield Hill to her own home. She was glad she'd had the chance of a chat with her old friend. For she didn't see him all that often nowadays. And yet when they were youngsters they had been almost inseparable.

"You're looking thoughtful," Mrs Lennox remarked, as her youngest daughter came into the kitchen.

"I'm trying to think if I have anything for Graham Shaw's fifty-fifty sale," Heather explained, running her finger around the bottom of her mother's mixing bowl. "His Cubs are out of funds."

"Really!" Molly Lennox exclaimed, giving the girl's hand a gentle slap, before she removed the bowl. "Licking out basins! And getting involved with Graham and his ploys. You'd think you were ten years old again!"

Before Heather could reply, the telephone rang and the young woman hurried through to the hall to answer it. She popped back into the kitchen five minutes later, her brown eyes shining.

"It was Barry," she told her mother. "I'm going over to his place tomorrow afternoon, because his mum wants me to show her how to make meringues. Then we're going out for dinner to the Old Barn Eating House. That's the place that has the great Country and Western group. I must just run upstairs and see what I have to wear."

As Heather's feet pattered upstairs, Molly Lennox shook her head. All thought of Graham and his sale had obviously flown out of the window!

Her eyes became dreamy as she began to lay the table for tea. Graham Shaw had always been such a nice lad. When he and Heather were young, he'd come around the Lennoxes so much he'd almost seemed like one of the family. And to tell the truth, at times he'd been a refreshing addition to their own four squabbling girls.

Molly had often wondered hopefully if he would in fact become one of the family eventually. But once they had left school and started work he and Heather had drifted apart.

And now Barry Davies had arrived on the scene to bring that special sparkle to Heather's eyes. Not that Barry wasn't a perfectly nice young man, too. It was just that . . . just that he wasn't Graham, Molly thought with feminine illogicality, as, hearing her husband, Tom, open the front door, she hurried to switch on the kettle.

WHEN Heather arrived at the Davieses' trim bungalow on Saturday afternoon, Barry welcomed her at the door with a warm hug, then led her through to the dining-room.

"Don't collapse," the blond young man warned Heather. "Mum took a mad turn this morning and started to clear out the loft. So all our family treasures are piled up in here."

"All our family rubbish, you mean!" pretty little Mrs Davies exclaimed, smiling a welcome to Heather from the chaotic muddle in which she was kneeling. "Half of this stuff will be in the dustbin by this evening, if I have my way!"

"She's ruthless," Barry informed Heather with a wink. "She's already thrown away my headless teddy bear and two battalions of toy soldiers."

"You always had far too much! That was your trouble!" Mrs Davies told her son. "Your father spoiled you when he came home on shore leave. Your grandparents spoiled you! And so did your aunts and uncles. Look at this, for example."

She lifted the lid of a large, dusty cardboard box to show Heather a red, streamlined train set, rather tarnished, but otherwise in good condition.

"This was in the window of Anderson's, the toy shop, Heather," she explained. "The little rascal went on about it for weeks. Finally his grandfather bought it for him. And do you know, he would never play with it, when he had friends in, in case they damaged it. So it was hardly used."

"There was another box that went along with it." Barry frowned, searching among the piles of boxes and containers that littered the floor. "It had stations. And model figures and animals. Did you find that?"

"Not yet," Mrs Davies sighed. "But I dare say I will."

"Oh, Barry!" Heather was staring at the train set, her eyes alight. And the next moment she was eagerly explaining to the Davieses about Graham's sale. "If you feel like parting with the train set . . ." she finished uncertainly.

"What a wonderful idea!" Mrs Davies exclaimed. "It ought to be

played with. Not stuck up there in the loft simply gathering dust.
But Barry was frowning.

"Hold on a bit, Mum!" he protested. "I'll have to think about it. Don't rush me!"

Mrs Davies, shaking her head despairingly at Heather, went off to wash her hands, before beginning her meringue-making lesson.

That evening as the young couple sat in the candle-lit restaurant sipping coffee after an excellent meal, Barry looked across at Heather, his blue eyes suddenly serious.

"The next time we come here, Heather," he said softly, "I hope it's to celebrate our engagement."

The blood rushed to Heather's cheeks and her dark eyes glowed.

"That sounds almost like a proposal," she murmured.

"Let's call it an advance warning." Barry smiled.

The young man had borrowed his mother's car for the evening, and he dropped Heather off at her gate at eleven o'clock. Down at the bottom of Northfield Hill she could see Graham Shaw slowly walking his old dog.

Tell-Tale Sign

MY husband feels he's getting old,
Though he looks so young to me.
But men go through this stage, I'm told,
And it is plain to see
The reason why he's feeling bad,
And seems bereft of fun —
The coalman has just called him Dad —
He used to call him son!

Avril Cowan.

"Don't forget about that train set, darling," Heather reminded Barry before she closed the car door.

Her boyfriend nodded and smiled, then blew her a kiss, before driving off.

As Heather walked up the moonlit garden path, she inhaled the sweet perfume of the blossom from the cherry tree in the garden, and suddenly she felt her heart was bursting with happiness.

She had been bowled over by Barry from the first moment they had met. And now he had more or less asked her to marry him. It was just all too good to be true.

Since the house was in darkness and her parents asleep, Heather tiptoed indoors and upstairs to her bedroom. But she was too happy and excited to feel sleepy. Instead she kneeled down on the window seat and gazed reflectively out at the star-filled sky.

Oddly enough, Heather had never yet thought seriously about marriage despite the fact that she was almost twenty-two. Her three sisters had all been mature, settled girls, who had married before they were twenty. But Heather, the "baby" of the family, had been quite different.

She had enjoyed spending her money on holidaying with the girls in the office and on buying clothes. She'd liked going to weekly discos.

Graham Shaw had been quite right when he'd teased Heather about having half a dozen boyfriends in a year. She'd never taken anyone or anything very seriously until Barry Davies had walked into the office and into her life. Then, in just a few weeks, she had known she was in love.

This past year had been truly magical. They had gone for trips down the river on golden summer evenings, driven out of the town in the autumn to see the countryside in all its glory and travelled north to ski in the Cairngorms over Christmas.

Heather had taken to Barry's mother right away. She was a warm, open woman with none of the possessiveness that mothers can sometimes show towards only sons.

Once Heather had asked Barry whether he had ever minded being an only child.

"No. Not really." He had smiled. "I always had plenty of friends. And, to tell you the truth, I think I enjoyed being spoiled by all our relatives."

In fact Barry had a very easy-going disposition, as Heather had found out. And if he did rather tend to like his own way, she soon found she could hold her own with him. Most of their tiffs so far had ended in laughter. But would it always be so, Heather wondered.

As the young woman looked out on the tranquil, moonlit garden, a little shiver ran down her spine. Marriage suddenly seemed a frighteningly decisive step, and she was filled with doubts. Was she ready for it? Did she love Barry as much as she thought she did? Could you really know another person after one short year?

As the questions buzzed round in her mind Heather suddenly realised she was feeling extremely tired. She pulled the curtains and switched on the bedside light. She would sleep on her problems, she decided. And perhaps by the morning some of them might have faded away.

THE following week was such a busy one in the office that Heather had little time to dwell on her personal problems.

Staff in Barry's department, too, were having to work overtime all week to get their returns in on time, so Heather saw comparatively little of her boyfriend. On the Friday afternoon when he popped in to see Heather for ten minutes, she remembered to ask whether he had made up his mind about the train set. But he shook his head.

In actual fact Heather had fully expected Barry to say he would take the train set over to Graham's at the weekend, and she was rather disappointed by his hesitancy. After all, it wasn't as though he were a model railway enthusiast or anything. He'd obviously never looked at the train for years.

To begin with, Heather had thought that Barry was resentful at his mother's gaily disposing of his property, and that this was why he'd held back. But now she was beginning to wonder. What was especially awkward was that she'd popped in one evening to tell Graham about the train set that would probably be coming his way. And Graham had been delighted.

Poor old Graham! He worked so hard for his Cub-pack, Heather thought as she finished work for the day and tidied up her desk. She would hate him to be disappointed, and right at the last minute, too.

SHARON DICKSON groaned as she put the cover over her type-writer and looked out of the window. It had been raining all day and the skies were grey.

"Whatever made me choose an early holiday this year?" she asked disconsolately. "If it goes on like this for the next two weeks I'll be sitting indoors twiddling my thumbs."

"Oh, this can't last," Heather said cheerfully. "After all, it is May."

"Yes. But it was still a mistake to take a May holiday when I wasn't going away." Sharon sighed. "There's nothing to do, Heather. Most of the excursions don't start until June. I hadn't thought of that."

"Never mind. I'm not going away either this year, Sharon. And when my turn comes round in July, I'll probably be moaning because all the excursions are booked up." Heather laughed.

"Well, at least you'll have Barry to run you around," Sharon remarked.

"Only for a week," Heather told her. "He had to take his second week in August."

Barry was working late again that night, and Heather took advantage of an evening at home to wash and set her hair. She was coming back downstairs to watch television, when the telephone rang, and she lifted it to hear her cousin, Marna Dick, on the other end of the line. The young schoolteacher sounded agitated and a trifle breathless.

"We're in a proper pickle at school, Heather," she explained. "Our party goes off on its Mediterranean cruise next Wednesday, and suddenly we're a teacher short! Miss Hawkins had a nasty fall from her moped this afternoon and she's landed up in hospital. We must have one adult to every twelve pupils, you see. And there isn't a single teacher or parent able to come!"

"Oh dear! What a shame, Marna!" Heather tutted sympathetically.

But her cousin broke in with a strained little giggle.

"It wasn't your sympathy I was phoning for, love," she explained. "It's you. I know you've got a passport. And we can rush your health insurance through. So is there the slightest chance of your being able to take your summer leave at short notice and come with us?"

"Me!" Heather gasped. "But . . ."

"You won't have to pay a penny, Heather," Marna went on hurriedly. "You'll be working your passage. And it's a fabulous cruise. Gibraltar, Tunisia, Italy, Greece . . ."

"Don't!" Heather protested. "I don't need any persuasion, Marna. It's just that my leave is booked for July this year. Only . . . there might just be a chance. Will you give me ten minutes and then I'll phone back?"

Half an hour later everything was miraculously settled, and Heather was sitting in the living-room with her parents, her eyes shining. Sharon Dickson had been more than willing to exchange leaves with Heather, and Mr Baxter, their boss, had been quite agreeable to it.

"What a chance!" Heather's grey-haired father commented, beaming at his pretty daughter. "A Mediterranean cruise dumped on your lap just like that! Nothing like that ever came my way!"

"Wait till Barry hears," Mrs Lennox chimed in. "He won't believe it! Will you ring him tonight?"

"No. It's rather late." Heather smiled. "I'll tell him when I see him tomorrow. I want to see the amazement on his face, anyway."

HEATHER met Barry at two o'clock on Saturday afternoon outside the town's Memorial Gardens. It was a mild day but the skies were still grey and overcast. She waited until they were sitting on the bench beside the goldfish pond before she excitedly told him her news and awaited his reaction.

"On Wednesday!" the blond young man repeated incredulously. "You leave on Wednesday!"

Heather nodded. She waited for Barry to congratulate her on her good luck. To say how fantastic it all was, as she certainly would have done, had their roles been reversed. Instead she saw his face cloud with disappointment.

"Well . . . aren't you happy for me?" she asked uncertainly, aware of a tight lump forming in her throat.

"Yes . . . Yes, of course," Barry replied, but his voice lacked conviction, and his eyes were far away.

He's upset because I've spoiled our July week together, Heather thought. That's what it is! How can he be so selfish?

"I'm going home, Barry," she announced, standing up abruptly. "I've got a splitting headache. Don't come with me. I can catch the bus at the corner."

"Are you sure?" Barry stood up, too, and made to take her arm but Heather moved away.

"I'll see you . . ." she began.

"Not tomorrow," Barry cut in quickly. "I've something on. And on Monday evening, too, I'm afraid."

"I see. Well, you can get in touch." Heather raised her hand in farewell, managing to smile despite the fact that hot tears were already pricking behind her eyes. Half an hour later in the safety of her own room they cascaded down her cheeks until her head was hot and throbbing and her pillow soaked.

HEATHER had so much to do during the next two days that it seemed impossible she could find time to think of Barry. But she did, constantly. And the longer she considered, the clearer it became to her what she should do.

She had thought her future with Barry was all tidily laid out. But in the past week she had suddenly seen her boyfriend in a new light. First of all there had been the incident of the train. And now had come Barry's reaction to the news of her holiday.

No matter how much she thought she loved Barry, she couldn't shut her eyes to this new aspect of him. And it didn't bode well for the future.

For didn't Mum always say that the secret of a happy marriage was give and take? And it certainly didn't look as though Barry were capable of giving.

No matter how much it hurt, she would have to finish with him before she found herself married to a selfish, inconsiderate husband.

On Monday Barry telephoned to ask if Heather could come over to the Davieses on Tuesday evening to have a quick cup of tea with his mother, since Mrs Davies wanted to wish her "bon voyage."

Heather agreed, knowing immediately that this was her opportunity. She would make a clean break, and then fall back on the diversions afforded by the cruise to help heal the wound.

BARRY picked Heather up at six-thirty on Tuesday evening, and as they drove down Northfield Hill they passed Graham unloading pieces of furniture from a van at his gate.

He grinned at Heather and she had an absurd urge to leap out of the car and appeal for his help as she had so often done, when she was a youngster and in some fix. But this time she was on her own. And she couldn't have been more aware of it as she finally stepped through the Davieses' front door.

Mrs Davies came out into the hall, beaming, and looked enquiringly at her son.

"Do you want tea before or after?" she asked.

"After," Barry retorted. Then he turned to Heather. "There's something I want you to see out in the garage." He smiled, taking her arm.

Too heavy hearted to feel even mystified, Heather let herself be led out of the kitchen door and into the Davieses' garage. There was a long workbench set up at one side, and it was towards this that Barry gently guided the young woman.

"There now!" he said with a hint of pride in his voice. "It's almost ready for your friend Graham's sale. What do you think of it?"

Heather, staring wide eyed at the bench, was speechless. The red engine and the wagons with their tarnished wheels had been totally resprayed so that they looked brand new. The rails were shining like silver. But not only that! There were tunnels and platforms, bridges and green fields. And the many toy figures of people and animals dotted around them were all gay with shiny, new paint.

"But it's beautiful, Barry!" she finally breathed. "Do you mean to say you've done all this?"

"He certainly has!" Mrs Davies cut in from behind them. "And don't I know it, Heather! He's been driving me mad! Out here at all hours trying to get it finished on time. And when you announced you were going off on your cruise tomorrow, he came home looking like a wet weekend, because he thought he wouldn't be able to show you the finished masterpiece. Great baby!"

"Well, I'd managed to keep it a secret . . . and I'd been looking forward so much to springing the great surprise," Barry admitted candidly.

"So that's why you looked so disappointed on Saturday!" Heather exclaimed. Then, unable to stop herself, she blurted out, "Oh, Barry! I'm so glad! So glad!" and flung her arms around his neck.

Arms entwined, the couple followed Mrs Davies back into the house and through to the sitting-room, where a plate of pink and white meringues adorned the centre of the coffee table.

"And now . . . I've something else to show you, love," Barry said gently. "Something rather special that Mum unearthed in the loft." And he drew a small, shabby, red leather box from his jacket pocket as his mother disappeared discreetly into the kitchen.

"Whatever is it?" Heather asked.

"My great-grandmother's engagement ring," Barry told her, opening the lid to reveal a dainty gold ring set with two sapphires and a small diamond.

"Oh, Barry! It's gorgeous!" Heather breathed.

"Will you try it on, love?" Barry asked softly. "If it doesn't fit we can always have it altered."

With a radiant expression Heather held out her hand and Barry slipped the ring on her finger. "A perfect fit!" he exclaimed.

"Perfect," echoed Heather, starry eyed, as Barry pulled her gently into his arms.

Fifteen minutes later Helen Davies stood gazing out of the kitchen window and listening to the young couple laughing and chattering in the sitting-room.

On the whole she was feeling extremely pleased with life. Particularly with the thought of having young Heather Lennox as a daughter-in-law, and being able to write and tell Derek, her husband, the good news.

But she did have one tiny complaint to make. For her first batch of meringues had turned out absolutely superb! And a compliment or two wouldn't have gone amiss. But that starry-eyed pair in there had scoffed the lot without a word, and hadn't so much as noticed what it was that they were eating. □

So Hard To Start Afresh

By Margaret Wyllie

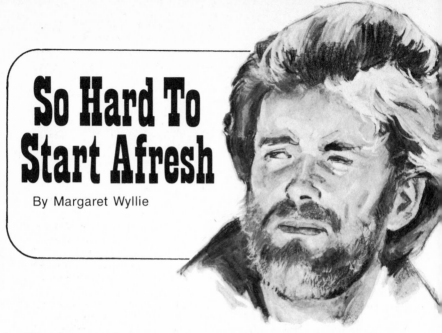

C AROL parked the library van in the lochside lay-by, and reached for her flask of coffee. It was almost two years since the first time she'd stopped here, but the spot still held the same fascination, though it was part of her routine now.

She'd been terrified, then, of some of the roads which her job obliged her to take — narrow and twisting with steep, sharp corners, dangerous gullies and rockfalls. She'd been anxious, too, that an English girl would perhaps be resented in this scattered Highland community.

She'd quickly got used to the roads though, and thanks mainly to Morag, she'd been accepted by most of the locals.

"They won't bite you," her friend had assured her brightly, when she'd raised the matter one morning. "They're slow sometimes about coming forward, but it won't take them long to get used to you."

Thank goodness, Morag hadn't been backward herself, when she'd noticed the library van. She'd pulled in at once and got out of her car, to "welcome Carol into the fold."

"I'm one of the district nomads too," she'd explained, her eyes sparkling with mischievous laughter. "The peripatetic music teacher, to be quite precise. It's a terrible mouthful, isn't it?"

Her kind gesture had brought a willing response, and they'd been very close friends ever since. If Morag had wondered why Carol had come here, she had never betrayed curiosity.

Carol's eyes clouded as she gazed at the mountains, stretching out to the distant Atlantic.

She had come here, hoping that a whole new life would help her forget Mark, but nothing, it seemed, could completely erase the nightmare of having to cancel all her wedding arrangements at the last minute.

16

"Please forgive me, Carol," he'd said in his letter, "You deserve someone better than me." Perhaps they all said that, to try to soften the blow. Not that it ever could.

He'd gone on to tell her about the girl he'd met at the new office he'd been transferred to.

From that moment Carol had just wanted to get away. She'd been working as a library assistant, so when this job came up it seemed the ideal opportunity.

S HE was still lost in thought when the small yellow car came over the breast of the hill.

"Sorry I'm late, Carol," Morag greeted her. "It's been one of those days, I'm afraid."

One of her pupils, a girl called Sally MacVicar, had accidentally got her violin smashed, and she'd been scared to go home by herself.

"It's really rotten luck." Morag sighed dejectedly. "It wasn't the kid's fault at all. They were pushing as usual, getting off the bus, and the case slipped out of her hand. The driver moved off, and a wheel went over it, before she saw where it was."

To make matters worse, Sally was one of Morag's most promising pupils, and she'd been entered for the schools' musical festival.

"There's only a couple of weeks to go, and I can't find another violin for her. She can borrow mine on the day, of course, but she needs one to practise with. Her grandpa could easily afford to buy her a new one, but there isn't much chance of that.

"He thinks she ought to be doing things on the farm, instead of 'wasting her time' as he puts it. He's a bigoted, stubborn old mule. It's a wonder to me that his housekeeper stands him."

Carol smiled involuntarily at her friend's hot outburst, although she sympathised with her problem. She didn't know the old man, but Meg Macfarlane, his housekeeper, was one of her regular borrowers. She had heard from her, about his flighty daughter and her early death, when Sally was only an infant.

"Some think he's ower strict," Miss Macfarlane had added, "but ye canna' blame him, considering. He's fond o' the lassie in his own kind of way, although whiles he's a wee bit awkward."

According to Morag, that was putting it mildly, but she was prejudiced at the moment. They'd had quite a row, when she'd taken Sally home.

"If he couldn't afford to buy a new violin I could understand, but Lochan Dhu farm is doing well. Anyone can see that for himself."

C AROL was no expert on farming, but it didn't need any specialised knowledge to see the difference between Lochan Dhu and the upland croft on the edge of the moor, which she called at the next afternoon.

Not that David Knight hadn't made great improvements in the time that he'd had Bencorrum. The ground had been cleared, drained and ditched, the cottage repaired and painted.

David Knight was even newer than herself to the district, and had come to the North from London. He'd apparently had some kind of illness and lost his job, and had decided to start afresh. He looked fit enough now though, as he came striding towards her with a spade slung over his shoulder.

"I'm sorry that book hasn't come yet," she told him, when he got within hearing distance. "I've brought another one though that's supposed to be better."

He gave her a friendly grin.

"Come and meet Victoria," he interrupted her cheerfully, disregarding her explanation. "She's still feeling strange, but she's missing her pals. She's been used to company, you know."

Carol turned her head slowly in the direction indicated and uttered a startled gasp.

A small white goat with malevolent eyes was regarding them both intently.

"She's really quite friendly," David reassured her, as the beast started trotting towards them. He was clearly delighted with his new acquisition, although to judge by the curl on Victoria's lips, his opinion was open to doubt.

"Come up to the house then, while I clean myself up. You can make us some tea while you're waiting."

Carol hadn't intended leaving the van, but the prospect of Victoria's undivided attention made her hastily change her mind.

What harm would it do, in any case, to go in for a minute or two? He must know by this time that her interest in him was confined to his choice of books.

He had asked her out, certainly, on several occasions, but he hadn't appeared unduly dejected when she turned down his invitations.

WHAT'S the problem then? Can't you find the caddy?" His voice made her start in confusion.

"Yes, I . . . no . . . I mean . . ." Colour stained her cheeks, as his eyes looked into her own. "I was thinking about Sally MacVicar," she said hastily. "Her grandfather farms Lochan Dhu."

At least that subject was safe, and it made conversation, without becoming too personal. There was a longish pause when she'd finished her story. Then David raised a quizzical eyebrow.

"Is the kid keen herself? If you think she is, there's a violin here she can have."

As he finished speaking, David crossed to the dresser, which ran the full length of the kitchen. Underneath the drawers were several large cupboards, which he proceeded to open at random. After several minutes, he unearthed an old case, and dumped it down on the table.

"It's only taking up room, here." He dismissed her protests. "I should have cleared up this stuff long ago."

He could certainly do with a bit more space, to judge by the cupboard's contents — cases and paint tins, boots and papers, old bits of rope and tools.

"Lachie's, not mine." His lips curved in a grin. "He won't need them now, I imagine."

The previous tenant, old Lachie, had been a bit of a ne'er-do-well. He had lived there alone, and after his death the croft had been sold as it was. He'd been a bit of a scrounger by all accounts. No-one had ever known him to work, but during the season he had tramped round the district in a moth-eaten plaid with a fiddle under his arm. The tourists enjoyed it, if the inhabitants didn't, which wasn't altogether surprising.

Like himself, no doubt, the old rascal's violin had probably seen better days, but it seemed ungrateful to refuse David's offer, and at least it was better than nothing.

Carol closed the case, and looked up with a smile.

"I'm sure Morag will be delighted."

I T was several days before they could meet, but the small yellow car was in the lochside lay-by when Carol got there on Friday morning.

The weather had changed in the interval and grey misty clouds hung over the mountains. The air was chilly and damp.

"Sorry I'm late." Carol lifted the violin from the passenger seat, as Morag climbed in beside her. "The road was pretty icy this morning."

Morag nodded absently, as she pulled off her gloves and eagerly opened the case.

"You're an angel, Carol . . ." Her voice suddenly faltered, as she lifted the instrument out.

In spite of herself, Carol bristled defensively.

"I *did* warn you, it wasn't that great," she began, "but . . ."

"It's a beauty, you dope! Much better than mine. You're boyfriend must be as daft as yourself, if he was just going to throw it away."

"He isn't my boyfriend," Carol corrected her sharply, "any more than that thing's a Strad!"

"I didn't say that it was," Morag eyed her thoughtfully, "but whatever you call him, he ought to be told, before I can give it to Sally. He could sell it, you know. I think it's worth quite a lot. I only wish that it wasn't!"

From her friend's point of view, that was only logical. Her pupil's interests came first, but David could probably do with the money. Carol bit her lip in vexation. She had a long day ahead and Bencorrum farm was a long way out of her route. On the other hand, it was in everyone's interests to settle this right away.

"I'll ring you tomorrow, and let you know," she told Morag, "I'll have to get a move on."

Carol made quite good time, in spite of several delays, but by the time she'd completed her calls in the glen, the mist was turning to sleet. The steep twisting road, never good at best, was treacherous in weather like this. Snow was lying up here, and the sullen sky gave promise of more to come.

It was cold in the van, in spite of the heater, and the lonely cottage was a welcome sight, as she rounded the final bend. She wouldn't quibble today about tea, she thought wryly, as she reached for the heavy knocker. He was taking his time, too, in opening the door. She banged it again, more loudly.

He must be at home, because his car was there, and he wasn't out in the fields. He might be working, of course, in the barn at the back.

The barn was empty, however, and the lean-to shed was equally unrewarding. All that remained was the ramshackle hut, which presumably housed Victoria. She approached it cautiously and peeped inside, before beating a hasty retreat.

Carol returned to the van and scribbled a note, explaining the situation. If his door was unlocked, which was usual here, she would leave the violin as well.

She was guiltily conscious of being an intruder, but she couldn't wait indefinitely, especially in weather like this. It would soon be dark and the wind was rising. She didn't want to be caught in a blizzard.

ENTERING the house, Carol closed the door quickly and went through to the kitchen. It was oddly cheerless and the fire had gone out. A pail of cinders stood in the hearth. Why hadn't he lit it, she wondered briefly, as she turned to the oil-clothed table.

It was set at one end and a half-cut loaf was lying out on the breadboard. It wasn't really peculiar, and yet she couldn't help feeling that something was wrong, that something unusual had happened.

Overcoming her scruples, she went through to the living-room and then glanced briefly into his bedroom and the bathroom. There was no sign of him.

As she made for the door Carol tripped over a tin of paint. The door of the dresser was ajar, and the can must have fallen out. Carol lost her balance and the keys for the van fell out of her outstretched hand.

As she stooped to retreive them, her eyes focused involuntarily on the cooker directly in front of her. A pan of half-cooked sausages stood on the hob, with an empty porridge pot beside it.

Carol straightened slowly. She'd been right, after all. Her misgivings came rushing back.

Why had he left in the middle of breakfast and not returned? It must be eight hours at least. It was after four now. And he hadn't taken his car. Her mind went round in circles, as she stared at the snowflakes swirling outside the windows and piling up on the sills.

Carol fought down her panic as she ran to the van, and fumbled to start the ignition. The engine was cold and it seemed to take ages before it suddenly roared to life. With a sigh of relief, she released the brake, and put the clutch in reverse.

She must get to the village, which lay at the head of the loch, to raise the alarm. But the forestry road, when it came in sight, seemed to offer a better solution. She knew there was a telephone box, just beside the fibrebrooms, about half a mile further on.

The road was narrower here, and though still used for access by the sawmill lorries, it wasn't in general use any more, since the highway had been improved.

Carol rolled down her window and reduced her speed till it was little more than a crawl. Ice had formed on the windscreen and she daren't take chances with the library van, no matter how impatient she was.

It was as well that she'd done so, for a moment later she was almost blinded by headlights swinging round a corner. Carol jammed on the brakes and her heart missed a beat as the van slid into a skid. With only inches to spare, both vehicles stopped, and the Land-Rover's passenger door banged open.

"You'll have to back up . . ." The voice broke off abruptly. The man standing outside was David! For an instant, he looked as surprised as herself, but it wasn't the place for long explanations, with his companion waiting for him.

"Wait here," David told her, once she was back at the junction. "I'll be back with my car as soon as I can, and you can follow me down to the village. We'll have a meal at the Inn before you go home. We may as well talk in comfort."

Without waiting to hear how she viewed his proposal, David jumped back into the waiting Land-Rover, leaving Carol confused and shaken. It would be simple enough to account for her visit, but what else could she say, without making herself seem a bit of a dimwit. Far from needing assistance, he must have been out all day with the mountain rescue team, searching for a missing climber.

The thought hadn't even crossed her mind, although it ought to have done, she supposed. Whatever else had been Lachie's, all that climbing gear that she'd noticed the other day wasn't.

I'M sorry I've messed up your evening like this. I'm afraid I . . . I jumped to the wrong conclusions."

They had finished their meal in the village inn, and were sitting in front of a blazing fire, drinking scalding-hot, freshly-ground coffee.

"I'm the one to be sorry, although I must confess I'm delighted to know that my absence disturbed you a little. I'm not *quite* so untidy, as a general rule, but I'd to leave in a bit of a hurry."

She was saved from replying by the innkeeper's wife coming in to remove the tray.

"The violin's out in the car." David got to his feet and stretched lazily. "That was my fault too, unloading it on you, without making its ownership clear. It just didn't strike me that you'd think it was Lachie's. His went to a jumble sale."

As he finished speaking, David picked up her coat and held it to warm at the fire. His hands looked no different from any other farmer's, Carol mused, unless you looked at them closely.

Calloused and strong, and tanned by exposure, there was little to show that he'd been a concert violinist, apart, perhaps, from the length of his fingers. He'd have still been a violinist if his left hand hadn't been badly injured in a car crash.

"It's OK now," he had told her at dinner, "but a couple of fingers don't work too well. The tendons got damaged or something."

He had dismissed the matter with a casual shrug, as though it wasn't

21

of any consequence. No hint of regret for his lost career, or the hardship of starting afresh.

"Why should I?" He'd grinned. "I might have been killed. I'm lucky to have another chance. And, as I'd always fancied trying my hand at crofting it seemed the ideal opportunity."

He was right, of course, but it wasn't as easy to forget the past as he had tried to make out. She knew, much better than he realised.

Carol pulled herself up with a frown. There was no comparison between their two situations, so why suddenly start to equate them?

"I can manage, thank you." She took her coat from his hands, as he held it out to assist her.

It was an ill-mannered snub, and she regretted it at once, although he didn't appear to notice. Why on earth had she done that, she asked herself irritably, as they walked to the car park in silence.

She hated being rude or offensive to people, and her rebuff had been entirely uncalled for. He hadn't meant her to feel like a weak-kneed fool, afraid of facing the future.

"There's a . . . a party, at the end of the music festival." She looked up at him hesitantly. "Just the Music Department and some helpers and friends. Perhaps you would like to come?"

For a long ghastly moment, there was silence. Then a grin slowly spread across his face.

"Nothing could keep me away," he assured her. "Not even a flock of Victorias!"

Sheer nonsense of course, but behind the banter he seemed genuinely pleased that she'd asked him. If he'd made some excuse, she would never have plucked up the courage again. Once had been bad enough.

She'd managed it though, and as the lights of the inn disappeared in the darkness, a glow of happiness stole into her heart, and she knew it was whole at last. The past was over and the future was waiting to fill her life with many more joys and sorrows. It might not be with David, but he had opened her eyes, and that was enough for the present.

She had done her best in the last two years to avoid getting hurt again, but the path she had chosen was just as stupid as the one that that climber had taken. You could lose your way by being over cautious, just as easily as by being reckless.

Light-heartedly, Carol headed for home. □

In the centre of Lincoln, standing on a 200-foot-high limestone plateau overlooking the River Witham, is majestic Lincoln Cathedral. Rising to 365 feet, it was built between the 12th and 14th centuries and is surrounded by mediaeval buildings. The city grew up on this site because of its strategic position. The Romans built a camp here and in 1068 William the Conqueror chose it as the site of a castle fortress. Lincoln is one of the most ancient sites in the realm and is rich in historic interest.

LINCOLN CATHEDRAL : J CAMPBELL KERR

Mother Knows BEST

TRUE, she had never actually met Mr Gavin Bell, but Anna Summers knew she disliked him already. Her mother kept going on about his brilliant university honours degrees, his appreciation of Continental cooking in fine restaurants — and so on.

But most of all she disliked the man for inveigling her mother into cleaning his flat next door. That really hurt.

Anna had worked hard, consciously seeking promotion in the D.I.Y. warehouse where she worked, so that her mother would no longer have to clean other people's houses.

What made it worse was the fact that her mother was like a new woman now, singing around their flat for the first time since her father had died two years ago.

She had even agreed at last to get rid of most of her heavy, old

by
Barbara
Cowan

furniture that didn't suit their modern flat, together with the old-fashioned patterned carpets. Now they were replaced with up-to-date, fitted units and self-coloured carpets, which Anna preferred.

She frowned a little as she carefully parked her car in front of the high-rise executive flats in East Kilbride. Frost crystals were starting to glisten on the road under the street lights as she made her way towards the immaculate entrance.

Anna noticed the caretaker had placed a little Christmas tree among his usual display of greenery. It looked really festive, and Anna felt her spirits rising, and her annoyance with the man next door abating a little. After all, her father used to insist his children made "Goodwill to all men" their motto in the weeks before Christmas.

B UT as soon as Anna opened the door of the flat her irritation returned. Her mother was nowhere to be found. No doubt she was next door, but her daughter was determined she wasn't going to enquire. She was unsure if she could be civil to Mr Gavin Bell when she finally met him.

"Is that you, Anna?" her mother called a few moments later, coming into the flat. "You're early, but Gavin said it was you. He can tell your footsteps going from the lift to our door." Mrs Summers beamed.

"Clever man," Anna murmured dryly, noting that her mother had now dropped the "Mr Bell," and was obviously on first-name terms.

"Oh, I've had such a day!" Mrs Summers exclaimed. "I took Gavin down to the supermarket to get a few things in for the festive season. You never saw such empty store cupboards, he's got no idea of how to feed himself at home. He eats out too much."

As they sat down to their supper, Anna listened as her mother happily recounted her shopping trip. Her animated face made Anna feel a little guilty about her dislike of their neighbour. Since he had moved in next door, two months ago, her mother's joy in life had been renewed and Anna could understand why.

Their two-bedroomed, centrally-heated flat was easy to clean, and it was difficult for her mother to find, suddenly, that she had time on her hands after a busy life looking after her husband and four children.

"I wondered if we should stay at home this year on Christmas Day, instead of going to our Craig's," Mrs Summers suddenly ventured.

Anna looked up in surprise. She had wanted to suggest this herself. The journey to Helensburgh from East Kilbride on Christmas Eve took such a long time, and if the weather was bad it was a nightmare. And with a new baby, she knew it would be a lot of work for her sister-in-law to have two overnight guests. But Anna was suddenly wary.

"Had you something else in mind?" she asked.

"Well . . ." her mother started. "Gavin has a brother who is coming to stay with him and they've no plans, so I thought since there's just the two of them, and there's two of us . . ."

"Have Christmas dinner with strangers!" Anna frowned at the thought. When her father was alive and the other three were at home, it was such a cosy family day.

25

"Shouldn't that be what Christmas is about — welcoming strangers? 'Goodwill to all men,' as your father used to say," Mrs Summers said sharply.

Anna opened her mouth to argue, but there was no answer to that. And the thought of being able to come home on Christmas Eve and just sit down and relax did appeal.

"Truth is, I want to get Christmas dinner ready in my own home again," Mrs Summers said to her daughter. "And you're usually so tired and out of sorts after all that driving and the Christmas rush in the warehouse. Hamish Cowan takes advantage of you, he makes you a real doormat."

"Just you make the arrangements, and I'll fit in with them," Anna said.

She would sit down to dinner with this unknown pair gladly, since the thought of it had changed her mother from the listless creature of the last two Christmases.

After the death of her husband, she had lost all her zest, especially at Christmas, a time her husband had loved. But now here she was, happily planning Christmas as her daughter remembered when she was youngest of the family.

ANNA had been the quiet, shy one, never as clever as her older sister Tricia, or her brothers, Andy and Craig. All married now, Tricia and Andy away in Canada, they had sailed through school and university, while Anna had to work so hard to get three "O"-grades.

She knew it disappointed her mother when she took a job with Mr Cowan in his Do-It-Yourself shop. But Hamish Cowan was ambitious and his business was expanding.

"I don't suppose you're thinking of taking on any more staff over the Christmas season?" Mrs Summers enquired a little later. "The caretaker was saying his daughter is looking for a holiday job."

"Nothing part time, but I think we'll have to take on a new boy for general duties round the place. And we don't need a university graduate for that," Anna said dryly.

Mrs Summers didn't answer. Her daughter was always disparaging about those with university training.

She looked thoughtful for a moment, but then brightened visibly. A vacancy for a boy — now that was a bit of luck!

Anna was a little amused when her mother made some lame excuse to go next door after supper. No doubt she would be washing dishes for their neighbour again.

NEXT morning, Anna Summers felt a familiar little thrill as she drove her car into the large car park of the warehouse.

There was tremendous satisfaction in seeing this building where she had helped in the planning and development of a thriving business.

"Excuse me, Miss Summers, I believe you might be looking for a boy for general duties." A thin, pale-faced boy confronted her.

"And what makes you think that you would be suitable?" she asked briskly, her eyes taking in his scrubbed face, neat belted anorak, and newly-cut hair. He had certainly made an effort to make himself presentable.

"I want to work and I'll work hard. I've got a good character reference from the headmaster," he said eagerly.

"What do they call you?" she asked.

"My name's Blair, but I'm usually called Bertie," the boy offered, his eyes shining as he sensed her sympathy.

"All right, Bertie Blair, we'll take you on temporarily over the Christmas period, and if you're suitable, we'll make you permanent."

During the next few days, Anna was impressed when she saw the boy scurrying around the place. He never seemed to be still.

Even Mr Cowan himself remarked on it as they stood in his office, looking through the glass partition to the floor of the warehouse. They could see young Bertie fetching and carrying, stopping occasionally to cheerfully direct a customer to the stand they were looking for.

"Strange, but that boy reminds me of you, always eager to please," Hamish Cowan remarked. Then he smiled contentedly.

"In just ten years we've built the business into this." He swept his arm over the vista of warehouse beneath them.

"How would you like to become my full-time partner, Anna?" he asked casually.

Full-time partner? Anna paused. Somehow it had a strange ring to it.

"Full-time partner in the business?" she murmured.

"And in my home," Mr Cowan said decisively. "I know I'm a good number of years older than you, but that shouldn't matter. We've made a good team here, so a marriage between us should work."

Anna was speechless. Hamish Cowan had never given the slightest sign of wanting to put their relationship on to a more intimate level. Yet, her mother often hinted that this was on his mind.

"I expect I've sprung this on you a bit, but I know you're not the silly romantic type. So give it some thought. I don't fancy a lonely old age." He patted her shoulder reassuringly, and went out of the office whistling.

A NNA stood for a moment, feeling slightly dazed. Not the romantic type! How little he knew, Her first proposal — and it came from a pleasant enough man, but with not a mention of love.

And yet, would she ever get another proposal? At twenty-six, there were no other young men in her life. There hadn't been time. She'd given her all to Hamish Cowan's business. Was marriage to him the next logical step?

For the rest of the day, Anna felt she carried a great weight of worry. The warehouse was decorated for Christmas and carols were piped through the loudspeaker system.

Customers thronged the aisles, but for once Anna did not share their expectancy. Surely this was not what one should feel after a proposal of marriage?

THE feeling of being distracted stayed with Anna, and she didn't see the young man running in the opposite direction towards the front entrance of the flats that evening.

Her head was down, and it caught him hard on the chin as they collided and he measured his full length in the foyer. The handle of her plastic shopper broke with the impact, and all the Christmas decorations she had bought rolled over the terrazzo.

"Oh dear," she gasped, dropping on her knees beside him, relief flooding through her as his eyes flickered open, and he slowly sat up, rubbing his chin.

"We'll have to stop meeting this way!" he murmured. "Gavin Bell is the name."

"Oh . . .oh . . .we're neighbours . . . I'm Anna Summers." Surely this couldn't be the man her mother was always talking about?

"Good grief! So you're Anna, the whizz-kid of business." He looked amazed. "You're not a bit as I imagined."

Then he started to slump forward, and Anna caught him in her arms, his head against her shoulder. Her mind was in a turmoil.

Imagine this being Gavin Bell. He was wearing jeans and a jerkin. She'd always pictured him middle-aged, dressed expensively in tailored lounge suits, with a haughty, scathing tongue. But really, it was rather pleasant to have his head cradled on her shoulder like this.

Then she heard running feet approaching the entry. She looked round and was surprised to see young Bertie Blair. Then his face fell as he saw Anna kneeling there.

"Gracious, Miss Summers, that's my brother! What's happened?"

Just then Anna felt the weight of the head being lifted off her shoulder.

"Why did you have to come now?" Gavin Bell said to the boy. "I was just beginning to enjoy that." He scrambled to his feet, putting a hand under Anna's elbow, drawing her upright.

Anna looked from one to the other, bewildered.

"See, I told you she was nice," Bertie said to his brother.

LIFE-LONG FRIEND

TICK tock! Grandfather clock.
Family's beloved old retainer.
Who sees the new-born child evolve,
from romping infant to radiant bride;
Marks the progress of the youth to
ultimate maturity, while parents' faces
gather shadows.
He shares the household's anxious
moments; hears laughter of the happy
days.
Night and day; day and night,
He tells the measured tread of
passing time;
Serenely chimes the hours, be there
azure skies or thundrous storm.
Dear life-long friend; companion of
the annals of the home through all the
changing hues of fortune,
Thy other name is constancy!
Were we as constant in our duty; as
faithful in the services we render – as
thou art!

Rev. T. R. S. Campbell.

"He didn't want to meet you, Miss Summers, because your mother is always boasting what a clever business woman you are."

They all went up in the lift together and Anna discovered that Bertie Blair was actually Blair Bell. Bertie was what he had been called in the residential home where the two boys had lived till quite recently, and both were quite matter-of-fact about being orphaned young.

By the time they reached their floor, the picture Anna had created in her mind about her next-door-neighbour had completely dissolved. How wrong she had been. This young man had feigned concussion to put his head on her shoulder. Such a thing had never happened to her before, and it was difficult to get used to.

Mrs Summers opened the door and looked startled at seeing the laughing trio on the doorstep. She stood aside and let them troop into the flat with the unravelled, gaily-coloured paper chains draped Hawaiian-style round their necks.

"So you've all met up at last," she murmured, pleased. Anna was giggling like a schoolgirl — she liked that. Somehow her daughter had never got the chance to act like that when she was in her teens. She was so shy and always working so hard, trying to prove herself.

"So that is how you knew about the job so quickly," Anna laughingly exclaimed to young Bertie. "I should have known my mother had a hand in it!"

Mrs Summers smiled secretly at this, she had known exactly what she was doing . . .

Later that evening, when the two young men had helped put up the decorations and returned to their own flat, Mrs Summers noticed Anna had become rather quiet.

"There's something bothering you, isn't there?" she queried.

Anna was about to deny it, then she sighed and told her mother about Hamish Cowan's marriage proposal.

"He doesn't want a lonely old age!" Mrs Summers almost exploded.

"You're only twenty-six, Anna. You want to look forward to something a bit more loving and romantic, with someone you can laugh and cry with through life's ups and downs. Not that Hamish Cowan . . ."

"I won't be accepting," Anna interrupted, and somehow her spirits rose as she made the decision. She knew she might have agreed almost out of habit because of the business, but after meeting Gavin Bell, she knew she couldn't.

For the first time in her life, she had glimpsed in him the fun, warmth and sense of loyalty she yearned for in her dreams. She knew now she could never settle for less, even if it meant never marrying.

I N the next few days, Anna discovered that for the first time in her adult life she couldn't concentrate on her work.

She found herself sitting at her desk smiling at some funny remark either Gavin or young Bertie had made the previous evening. Or trying to swallow a lump in her throat, remembering how they spoke, quite matter-of-factly, about the years in the home.

"Give the authorities their due, they always tried to keep us together," Gavin had admitted the night before, as they all sat drinking mugs of coffee in her mother's flat.

"They even tried to get us fostered, but no one fancied taking on two brothers with a ten-year age gap between them, and besides, we didn't want to be separated."

"Yes, we used to make solemn promises about it." Bertie nodded. "Remember, Gavin, you used to tell me how you were going to get a house with a garden for the two of us when you grew up."

"Yes, and we were going to have a cow for milk, chickens for eggs, and a sheep to get wool to make our clothes." Gavin laughed, shaking his head at their innocent dreams.

"Yet, the one thing I'll always remember best was one Christmas." Bertie looked at his brother seriously. "You told me the story of Bethlehem, of how the family in the stable on Christmas night were just like us — they had no home either. I've never forgotten how it comforted me."

"That's so true," Mrs Summers put in. "My husband would have liked that, he was a great one for trying to understand the real spirit of Christmas." Her eyes misted as old memories of Christmastime spent with her husband flooded back.

THERE was an awkward silence, then Gavin stood up briskly. "I almost kept my word, too." He grinned. "We've got a home. No garden, or cow, sheep or chickens, but it's comfortable!" He looked at Anna, laughter glinting in his eyes. "Come on, it's time I showed it to you . . ."

Anna got up, smiling. She was getting to know Gavin and sensed he had some surprises in store for her.

"Oh, yes, he's got it really lovely." Mrs Summers beamed at her daughter, her momentary sadness disappearing.

Anna looked at the three smiling faces, wondering just what was in store in Gavin's flat. But when she went next door and crossed the threshold, at first she was startled. Then she saw the funny side, and laughed until her sides ached.

Gavin's flat was exactly like their own had been till two months ago!

"When I moved in, I had next-to-no furniture," Gavin explained. "Your mother told me she was refurnishing and sold me her old stuff cheaply, otherwise it would have taken me years to furnish this place."

"Not if you'd learn to cook instead of spending so much money on eating out," Mrs Summers admonished him, smilingly. "Have you used that old cookery book yet?"

"Oh, yes, we had beans on toast tonight, and I hardly burnt the beans at all!" Gavin chuckled.

"Don't you believe it — he made that casserole on page thirty, and it was smashing!" Bertie said, appreciatively. "But I *am* looking forward to a real Christmas dinner, with us all together." He looked eagerly at the two women. "Just like families do it," he added, with a boyish grin.

Gavin rubbed his hands in anticipation.

"I'm looking forward to the mistletoe," he declared cheekily. "Then I can kiss two certain ladies soundly, without getting my face smacked!"

Anna giggled, and her mother couldn't hide the pleased smile which lit up her face.

It was later, in their own flat, that Anna tackled her mother about the mistaken image of Gavin she had given.

"Oh, I told you just enough." Mrs Summers sounded complacent. "I knew you'd hit it off when you finally met!"

D URING the days before Christmas, Anna purposely avoided being alone with Hamish Cowan. It was quite easy because the festive rush was on and everyone was busy. Yet, about five o'clock on Christmas Eve, the crowds thinned out suddenly and the aisles of the warehouse were deserted. Miss McLaughlin from the office met her.

"I think Mr Cowan is looking for you." She looked at Anna coyly. "He's been saying that you two might be Mr and Mrs before long."

Anna felt a surge of panic sweep over her. Fervently she wished her employer hadn't mentioned the possibility to anyone. Her refusal would be all the more embarrassing for him, she told herself.

"He's a great one for a joke, isn't he?" she murmured airily, and hurried into the stockroom for the sole purpose of gathering her wits about her.

Anna came on Bertie in the back recesses of the stockroom. He looked anxiously into her face.

"There're rumours flying about . . ." he began, his face flushed with embarrassment. "You're not going to marry Mr Cowan, are you?" he blurted out.

"No!" Anna shook her head.

"Oh, I'm glad! Our Gavin says he would like you as his steady girlfriend. Last night he told me you're the kind of girl he'd like to marry." Wistfully he added, "It would be the best Christmas present I could have — then your mother would be my granny, sort of, wouldn't she?"

"Indeed, she would insist on it!" Anna cried, and gave him a quick hug.

"Will you be long?" Bertie grinned. "Our Gavin is waiting at your car with a big bunch of mistletoe." This piece of news made Anna giggle delightedly.

"Tell him to wait. I've got a little business to finish with Mr Cowan, then I'll be right out."

A little later, as she flew down the steps from Hamish Cowan's office, Anna remembered how her father had always said Christmas was a time for new beginnings.

Through a window on the staircase she glimpsed Gavin waiting at her car and her heart leapt.

His presence there seemed to Anna to be a perfect symbol of the new life of loyalty, love and laughter she had always dreamed about.

This Christmas, Anna's dreams would become a reality. □

Dreams Can Come True

by Grace Macaulay

"L ETTER for you, Joanne." Linda tossed a blue envelope across the breakfast table, adding happily, "And one for me too."

Linda ripped open her envelope, and as she opened out the bulky letter she absent-mindedly reached for a piece of buttered toast and chewed it while she read.

Joanne picked up her letter and stared at her mother's handwriting with a strange feeling of dismay. She didn't want to open it — not yet, not while last night's dream was still lingering in her mind.

She and Donald had been hand in hand, laughing as they climbed among the birches. There had been soft clouds beneath their feet as they'd followed the winding path to the upper falls of Moness.

She could feel the warm strength of Donald's hand in hers as they'd gazed together at the magnificent cascades of foaming water thundering over the stones.

When she'd looked at Donald, he was looking at her. But when she'd spoken his name he hadn't heard her. He'd given her no answer at all. He just looked at her with that sweet, wistful smile at the corners of his lips.

SHE turned the letter over, wishing she could leave it unopened until that evening. The dream would have faded by then. But if she did, Linda would be sure to comment and ask questions. Better open it now and get it over with. The worst that could be in it would be the news that he was already married.

Her heart was pounding as she scanned the two pages for a glimpse of Donald's name. But there was no mention of him and she began to read more calmly.

Linda had already finished her letter and she pushed it back into the envelope.

"My parents want me home next weekend for a party," she announced.

Joanne looked up, surprised.

"So do mine."

"It's my father's birthday," Linda said. "What's yours in honour of?"

"My parents' silver wedding," Joanne answered, adding, "it's a sort of spur-of-the-moment party, my mother says."

"Always the best kind," Linda said, smiling. "What are you going to wear? I think I'd better have something new — although there's the fare home and Dad's birthday present to budget for as well. Maybe I could cut out lunches all week."

But, occupied as she was with her own plans, Linda couldn't fail to notice something evasive in the other girl's expression.

"What's the matter?" she asked. "Aren't you pleased about the party?"

Joanne folded the letter with elaborate care.

"Not specially," she replied quietly.

"But you'll be going, surely?" Linda frowned.

Joanne gave a small shrug.

"I don't know. I don't suppose they'd miss me," and to her horror, she could hear her voice shake. It was almost as if she had said aloud, I can't go because Donald might be there . . .

There was a long, strained silence. Linda knew about Donald. But she'd thought recently that Joanne was recovering from his betrayal. Now she realised that she'd been mistaken and she longed to be able to think of some comforting remark.

However, it was Joanne who broke the silence.

"It isn't very long — three months, two weeks and three days," she said gloomily. "But in some ways it seems like an eternity."

Softly, sympathetically, Linda said, "No, it's not long, considering all the years before."

"All in all it was sixteen years." Joanne spoke with a hint of bitterness. "Did I ever tell you that he held my hand on our first day at school?"

Linda shook her head, looking at her flat-mate thoughtfully. "You just told me that he called off the wedding you'd been planning for years — because of your cousin." Then she added, awkwardly, "I gathered you didn't want to talk about it."

"I still don't want to talk about it." Joanne sighed wearily. After a lengthy pause, she went on, "My cousin Sandra's mother was my mother's bridesmaid. There's no possibility of Sandra not being at the party. Which means that Donald will too." And she faltered over his name.

Again, Linda was at a loss for words. She pushed back her chair from the table and went to fetch the teapot.

As she refilled their cups, she found herself, for the first Saturday in her life, wishing that this was a working day. Somehow or other she knew that they would be spending the best part of the day agonising about Joanne's dilemma. Which was a pity, because Linda had planned to spend the day mostly thinking about Bruce Esplin; and making herself beautiful for their date tonight.

L INDA sat down at the table to drink her tea. But as she lifted the cup to her lips, three thoughts raced into her mind in rapid succession. First she wondered whether she should ask Bruce to come home with her next weekend to the party. Secondly, she remembered that tonight was a double date — Joanne was going out with Bruce's friend Steven for the third time. And finally, her cleverest thought of all which she voiced with extreme caution.

"If you asked Steven to go to the silver wedding party with you, I'm certain he'd be delighted." As Joanne looked at her with a spark of light showing through the despondency in her eyes, Linda went on eagerly, "You'd be killing two birds with one stone — making your parents happy, I mean, and letting everyone else, including Donald, see that you're not pining away!"

Slowly, pensively, Joannne replied.

"Yes, that could be the answer." But a shadow crossed her face as she added doubtfully, "I suppose."

In her own mind she'd been considering telephoning her mother. It wouldn't be easy to confess that her cheerful letters home had been written mainly out of pride. Admittedly she'd wanted to reassure her parents, to answer the anxious questions which she could always read between the lines of their letters.

Also, she'd had the idea that if she tried hard enough she would heal the painful wounds which had been inflicted on her heart. Surely she'd be able to make her mother understand? It's too soon, Mother, she would say, I'm not quite strong enough; my courage isn't equal to seeing them together.

But now, here was Linda suggesting an alternative course of action. A tempting idea, far preferable to making the humiliating telephone call, she thought. And yet it didn't seem quite right. She didn't know why . . .

"Will you think about it?" Linda asked. "Seriously?"

Joanne nodded, sighing. She sipped her tea slowly before replying. "Yes, I'll think it over."

Linda gave her a searching look.

"You and Steven always seem to find plenty to talk about," she said quietly.

"Always?" Joanne's chin rose. "What do you mean always? I hardly know him!"

"Sorry! Sorry! I didn't mean anything at all!" Linda put her hands up, smiling.

The angry colour faded from Joanne's face and her lips finally twitched into a smile.

"You're right, of course," she agreed. "We always have lots to say — ideas to exchange."

"Similar ideas . . . mutual interests . . ." Linda raised her eyebrows mischievously.

Joanne nodded pensively.

"Steven's a very relaxed sort of person. I should imagine he'd get along with anyone."

"Oh," Linda said, but the look on her face was eloquent.

"Sorry to disappoint you." Joanne's eyes twinkled. "But I'm not interested in him — not in the way you seemed to be hoping." Then she added briskly, "Now let's clear up these dishes. It's my turn to go to the launderette so I'd better get a move on otherwise I'll have to queue for a machine."

Linda got to her feet reluctantly.

"And it's my turn to clean the flat," she said. After a moment, she asked hesitantly, "You have enjoyed going out and about a bit, haven't you? I used to worry about you staying in the flat night after night."

"I know you did," Joanne answered. Her brow furrowed as she replied to the original question. "At first, I only went out because you were so insistent. But now that I think of it — you were right. I feel much more confident these days; the more people I meet the easier it becomes. I'm not a timid wee village girl any more!"

BUT in spite of her brave words, Joanne knew that she was far from being the sophisticated, self-assured person she'd like to be . . . otherwise she'd have had the stamina to go home next weekend.

Would it be easier if she asked Steven to accompany her? All day the question flitted backwards and forwards in her mind but she still hadn't reached a decision by the evening.

It would have been so easy to ask him. The question hovered on her lips many times during the course of the evening. But when Steven said to her, "You're quiet tonight, Joanne, there's something on your mind, isn't there?" the right words didn't come.

Instead, she summoned up a smile and told part of the truth.

"It's my parents' silver wedding next week and I'm wondering what to buy for them."

"I bought mine a silver rosebowl and a bunch of red roses."

Steven answered promptly. "It wasn't very original but I think they were pleased."

"Did anyone else give them the same?" Joanne queried.

"No," he said.

"Then it was original!" Joanne told him.

"Unique, I suppose," he agreed. And they laughed companionably, affectionately.

"Anyhow, I'll copy your idea," Joanne said, "if you don't mind."

He didn't mind. And after a moment, their talk switched to another topic. Joanne was careful not to mention the silver wedding again . . . tomorrow she would ring her mother and make her excuses.

Welcome To Spring

LEAVES appear on the trees again
Little green shoots lift their heads.
Creatures, from long hibernation
Rise sprightly from their beds.

Sweet is the scent of the blossom
And fragrant the flowers of spring;
The laughter of children is mingled
With the sounds of birds on the wing.

Warm is the sun in the morning
As gently it touches the earth;
Bringing the promise of springtime,
And the wonder of Nature's rebirth.

Eileen E. Davis.

NEXT day, however, before Joanne had an opportunity to phone, two unexpected visitors arrived at the flat — Mr and Mrs Macdonald who had once lived next door to them in the village.

"Your mother was on the phone to us last night about the party," Mrs Macdonald explained after the first greetings were over, "and when she told me you were here, living and working in Glasgow, I could hardly believe my ears. Fancy you never getting in touch with us!"

Joanne blushed as she searched for an excuse.

"It's taken me a while to find my way around. When you're working . . . you know how it is."

Suddenly the older woman looked embarrassed, as if she'd only just remembered Joanne's reason for leaving home. "Anyway," she said swiftly, "we thought we'd call in on our way back from church — to make arrangements for Saturday. There's no need for Joanne to bother about the bus, I told your mother. She can easily travel with us, there's plenty of room in the car."

Joanne had no option but to agree and express her gratitude. She couldn't let them see how her heart quailed at the prospect. Pride wouldn't let her.

After they had gone, Linda turned to her with a sympathetic look.

"Didn't you ask Steven?" she enquired.

Joanne shook her head.

"It's never good to make use of someone. I'd have felt guilty afterwards. And apart from that, it wouldn't have been fair to give

Steven any wrong idea, at least not yet. I realised last night that I do like him, you see."

"But if you like him . . .?" Linda looked perplexed.

Joanne struggled to explain.

"We have a pleasant, easy-going friendship right now. Maybe sometimes we'll get, sort of, closer. But not if I deliberately use him as a morale booster. He would guess, you know. And he'd be hurt. Then we'd never have any way of getting back together."

"Yes, I see that," Linda agreed. She continued, "I suppose a man would inevitably attach some significance to being invited to a girl's home for the weekend."

Some quality in her tone, jolted Joanne out of her own concerns.

"You mean you invited Bruce? What did he say?" she asked.

"He said . . ." Linda paused and sighed dramatically, "he said, he loved me — and would he ask my father a certain question. Naturally, I said — no — he must ask me! And I said yes, yes and a hundred times yes!"

Linda's eyes were sparkling brilliantly as she went on to predict how delighted and astonished her parents would be.

The following evening after work, Linda and Bruce bought the engagement ring and returned to the flat with a celebration bottle of champagne.

But although Joanne was genuinely happy for them, she left them alone as soon as politeness allowed and escaped to the solitude of her own room.

All week she found herself constantly burdened by an uneasy, brooding apprehension. Then on Saturday morning when she was waiting for her promised transport, she was suddenly aware of an amazing feeling of elation. She had lived through every kind of meeting with Donald in her imagination. Sometimes she'd wept; other times she'd been unable to speak — she'd even fainted in one of her fantastic, vividly embroidered scenes. Now, it was if they were all out of her system; leaving her cool and poised and completely devoid of emotion.

THAT evening, at the party, when Joanne's eyes met Donald's she was ready. Giving a distant nod and a cool half-smile, she turned away to talk to someone else. But she had no way of controlling the stab of anguish at her heart, nor the jangling nerve ends which were raw with pain.

It wasn't until much later that she realised he was alone. In a quiet moment her mother told her, "Donald and Sandra didn't last long together. They split up weeks ago. She's away working in a hotel in Edinburgh."

Joanne was too taken aback to answer. And her mother, as if sorry that she had spoken, went on hurriedly to thank Joanne for the present she had brought.

"It's something I've always wanted, a silver rosebowl," Mrs Thornton said happily, "and it was so thoughtful of you to bring roses

37

too. Ours won't start coming into bloom for another week or two. Having recovered her composure, Joanne smiled.

"I remembered that," she said, "and I thought what's the good of an empty bowl? But it was actually an idea I got from somebody else — I've told you about Steven in some of my letters, haven't I?"

On the drive back to Glasgow, she sat quietly in the back of the car, drowsily letting the events of the day drift through her mind.

"Bring him home to meet us," her mother had said about Steven. And she'd answered vaguely that she might do so. But now, she knew she never would. Friends they could be. But nothing more — never anything more.

Much later, when she finally lay down in bed, she closed her eyes and let herself think of Donald. It had been easy to avoid him — for he'd made it obvious that he was avoiding her. Except for that first meeting of their eyes, there had been no contact between them.

Scalding tears burned their way under her eyelids on to her face and she shuddered convulsively. He hadn't even asked her to dance.

I N the morning, she woke early and ate a solitary breakfast. But she was restless and unwilling to stay all day cooped up in the flat.

If she'd been at home she would have gone out for a walk on the hills . . .

I'll go out for some Sunday papers, she decided. Even a short walk in the air would be refreshing.

Ten minutes was all it took, and she climbed the stairs to the flat wondering how she would fill the rest of the day. She'd have to do something. She definitely wouldn't allow herself to sit around moping. Once and for all she must put Donald out of her mind.

She looked up and, as if she was seeing a picture coming to life, there was Donald standing outside her door. Wordlessly, she stared at him, clutching the newspapers tightly against her to steady the rocking beats of her heart.

"I couldn't speak to you yesterday — not in front of everyone," he said in a low, uncertain voice.

Waiting for her to answer, his eyes seemed to be pleading with her in a humble, apologetic appeal. Never before had she seen such an expression of deep yearning on his face.

"Donald . . ." she said in a tremulous whisper.

Silently he took her in his arms, and as they held each other tightly Joanne fleetingly recalled her dream of walking hand in hand with him to the Birks of Aberfeldy and climbing all the way up to the Falls of Moness.

But this was no dream. His arms around her were real and true, his lips against hers were fierce and passionate and she was responding with an eagerness which was new and exciting.

Yet it didn't seem as if they were making up for all the wasted days they had been apart . . . their embrace was utterly new and wonderful. It was like another love, another dream that they would cherish for ever. □

by Margaret Johnston

When The Baby's Born

J EFF BAKER kissed Karen gently as they paused outside her gate.
"Hey! Haven't you a home to go to," he teased.

But Karen didn't return his smile, instead she fastened her arms
tightly round him and laid her cheek against his jacket.

"It's early yet," she assured him.

Jeff lifted her face with firm fingers, but he kept his voice light.

"Look, I don't want your father after me. He's bigger than I am."

"Oh, Jeff!" The girl's voice was full of exasperation. "You know
Dad never worries when I'm with you. I don't want to go in yet."

As she snuggled closer, Jeff couldn't help the thrill of happiness which
ran through him.

He had known Karen almost all his life, but it was only during the last year that he had noticed that she had grown up. She wasn't the leggy, aggravating child who had dogged his footsteps throughout the years any longer.

But Karen was sixteen to his twenty years and he wouldn't have been surprised if her father had objected to his taking her out.

When the subject was broached Mr Bristow eyed him closely.

"I've known you all your life, young Jeff, but Karen's not much more than a child. You mind that, Jeff Baker."

Jeff had nodded, blushing under the older man's stern gaze. But then Mr Bristow had laughed and slapped him on the shoulder, and invited him to have a glass of his home-brewed beer, and Jeff knew he had an ally.

MAYBE your father doesn't worry," he said now. "But it is getting late."

He released his hold, but Karen stayed pressed against him and he sensed there was something more than a mere reluctance to leave him.

"You're not still upset about your mother, are you? I thought you'd be used to the idea of her having a baby."

Karen seemed to give a little shudder.

"I don't think I'll get used to it. At their age! It doesn't seem right."

Jeff forced a laugh. "Their age! Your parents are hardly in their dotage. And, if they don't mind, I don't see why you should."

"Oh, they don't mind. They're positively besotted about the whole thing, but, but . . ." Karen stuffed her hands into her pockets and turned away. "If you can't understand how I feel . . .!"

"Of course I can understand. I suppose your Mum does, too. You said she was a bit . . . well, that she didn't like telling you. But it won't be so bad once the baby comes. And just think, you'll maybe earn some more pocket money by baby-sitting."

Karen pulled away, her face clouded with anger.

"It's just a joke to you, isn't it? That's what it is to everyone who knows me. They all look at me, and laugh, and say things. It's — it's ridiculous!"

"Are you sure you're not just jealous? Maybe you think you'll get your nose pushed out. After all, you've been Mummy's pet for sixteen years."

Karen's eyes blazed at him.

"What a thing to say! Of course I'm not jealous. Anyway, Mum never spoiled me as you're implying. I think you're mean to say such things. You're supposed to love me."

"I do, you know I do. But, love, the baby's going to be born. You've just got to accept it."

"But I don't have to like it, do I?"

Jeff watched Karen run the few yards to her own garden gate, and disappear inside the house, before he walked up to the other end of the street where he lived. There was time, he thought. Maybe with time Karen would get used to the idea of a new brother or sister.

When The Baby's Born

K AREN closed the door behind her and leaned against it, trying to control her tears. She could hear her father pottering around in the kitchen and the jingle of some advertising slogan being sung in the sitting-room. Clearly Dad was making the hot drink he brewed each night for her mother.

She couldn't let him see her like this. But, as she turned to the stairs, her father opened the door.

"That you, love? Want some chocolate?"

"Yes," Karen made herself reply normally. "Yes, please. I won't be a minute." She dashed upstairs and splashed cold water over her hot cheeks. Despite what Jeff said, she did love her parents, she didn't want them to guess what she was feeling.

Putting a bright smile on her face, Karen walked into the sitting-room.

Mary Bristow saw the brightness of the smile and recognised its falseness.

"Leave her alone," Brian had always said when she voiced her doubts. "It's been a bit of a shock, she'll come round."

Mary loved him dearly for his support and understanding, but she didn't think he quite understood about Karen.

Young people were supposed to be so uninhibited, so knowledgeable, she thought. Perhaps it's our fault. We give them the facts but do they understand the emotions which go with them?

But sadly, she had to realise that Karen was young and vulnerable, and she tried not to force the coming baby, and all it entailed, into her daughter's life.

If Brian commented on the new dress she was wearing, Mary turned his remarks aside, but there was no way she could prevent the proud father-to-be from teasing her.

"Are you sure you're not having twins?" Brian would ask, making a great pantomime of leaving Mary room to pass him.

And when he was brushing his thinning hair he would grin at his reflection, and console himself.

"Never mind, old lad. There'll be two of us who'll be a bit thin on top in a few months."

Karen watched her father's attempts to disguise his lack of hair and a kind of disgust filled her.

He was too old! Of course he and Mum must have been in love once, just as she and Jeff loved each other. Perhaps they, too, had felt the tumultuous feelings which swept over her when Jeff held her in his arms. But that should be over now.

Dad was getting a paunch, and Mum's hair was streaked with grey. Their hearts couldn't beat faster, their breaths catch in their throats just at the sight of each other, as hers did when Jeff walked down the avenue to meet her.

Why, Mum didn't even seem to care what she looked like! Why didn't she buy some of these new maternity designs? Just because those horrible smock things had been the sort of clothes she'd worn before, it didn't mean she had to proclaim her condition to the whole world. It seemed almost indecent.

"Don't you mind Dad seeing how you look?" Karen had ventured one day. Her mother had smiled slowly.

"I rather think he knows how I look," she said quietly, and then mischief had sparkled in her eyes.

Karen had never mentioned the way she dressed again, and the coolness between them increased.

Now, with the quarrel with Jeff fresh in her mind, Karen wished she could talk to her mother as she'd always been able to do.

She sat drinking the chocolate her father had brought in to her and kept her eyes averted from her mother's.

"Had a nice evening?" Mary asked, and Karen wondered if traces of her tears were still visible.

"Mmm," she murmured. "But we went to a film. It was all sad, a real weepy," she said brightly, lifting her face defiantly.

If only things had been the same. Of course she was too big to sit on her mother's lap, as she had as a child, but how she longed to feel her mother's arms around her and her voice telling her everything was going to be all right.

Maybe I am jealous. Maybe Jeff was right, Karen thought. But deep down she knew it was more than that.

THE weeks passed and soon Mary was packing her case, ready to go to the hospital at a moment's notice.

"I'm glad they let you out after a couple of days," she told Karen. "Let you out." She laughed shakily. "Makes it sound like jail. But I do want to get home quickly. Then the baby really seems to belong to you. Watching everyone else fuss about them, they never actually feel yours."

But despite her ideas, Brian hadn't been too keen on her taking over quite so rapidly, and after a lot of argument Mary had agreed to have some help during those first days at home.

When Karen woke one night to the sound of banging doors and hurried footsteps, and her father's frantic whispers, she knew the moment had come. She lay rigid, pretending that she hadn't woken, hoping no-one would come to tell her that her mother was leaving.

But listening to the near panic in her father's voice, she felt ashamed, and shrugging on her dressing-gown, she crept down the stairs.

Mary was sitting on the little seat beside the telephone, her case beside her.

"Sorry we woke you, love. Anyone would think no-one ever had a baby before. Your dad's in a terrible state. Listen to him, he can't start the car."

"Shall I see what I can do?" Karen smiled.

Mary put out a hand and gripped hers.

"I think he'll manage," she said slowly. "Just stay here a moment."

Karen felt the fingers dig into her palm and kept her mind firmly on the falsely revving engine until it started.

"There! Dad's managed it." She shifted her grip until she held her mother's arm. "Come along. You'd better be off."

When The Baby's Born

Her bed was cold when she crawled back under the covers and it was a long time before she slept again. Tomorrow there would be another member of the Bristow family. It was a thought which chased sleep away.

She received the news of her baby brother with a strange feeling of not belonging. It was almost as if it had nothing to do with her.

"How's Mum?" she forced herself to ask, and watched the relief flood into her father's eyes.

"She's fine, leastways, she says she is. The doctor agrees, so I suppose she must be," he allowed reluctantly. "But she's tired. I'm glad I insisted on Mrs Grant coming in. Can't think why they send them home so soon," he grumbled.

He prowled the house restlessly. Clearly, to him, it didn't seem like home without Mary's presence.

The day her mother was due home, Karen walked slowly up the avenue. A twinge of something like excitement curled in her stomach as she thought of the new baby, and she recalled the envy of her schoolfriends.

"They're so sweet," one after the other had cried. "So soft and lovely."

LIGHT OF THE WORLD

*T*HE floodlight, the lamp and the candle, these three, but the least of these is the candle. Is not the humblest measure of light one-candle power?

Switch off the lights in the room, that the berry-red candles of Christmas may mellow the festal table with their little golden light.

Switch off the lights in some vast hall. In the great deep darkness a single candle sheds a surprising halo of light.

"Light of the world," Christ calls us. Some blaze as floodlights; shine as lamps. But others are just Christ's candles; one-candle power.

Yet on some lonely soul in darkness of spirit, the candle of a kindly word, a thoughtful deed, can shed great light!

Rev. T. R. S. Campbell.

Karen hadn't said much except to remind the other girls that babies cried, too.

Now she pushed open the front door and stood hesitantly in the hallway. She could hear someone in the kitchen but guessed it wasn't her mother. Glancing upwards towards the closed bedroom door, she crept through into the kitchen. Mrs Grant turned from the sink.

"You'll be Karen. My! You're every bit as bonnie as your mother said you were."

Karen laughed. "Oh, Mother!" she said.

"Ay, she thinks a lot of you. It's been Karen this and Karen that, since the moment I arrived."

"How is she?" Karen asked, partly to hide her embarrassment.

"Why don't you go and see for yourself?" The keen eyes seemed to be able to see inside Karen's head.

"I was just going to. I wanted a drink," she excused herself.

43

But though she sipped the water slowly, she knew the moment couldn't be postponed any longer, and, at last, she moved to the kitchen door.

"Isn't Mum sleeping?" she asked, anything to put off the meeting. Mrs Grant laughed.

"She'll not get much chance of that with your father around. He can't stir from her side. They're sitting there making sheep's eyes at each other."

Karen had thrown her a startled look. Mum and Dad? It didn't seem possible. They kissed, quickly and inexpertly, when Dad went to work. Dad often ruffled Mum's hair and she punched his increasing tum playfully. But sheep's eyes!

K AREN went upstairs, opened the bedroom door and instantly saw that Mrs Grant had been right. Her father was sitting uncomfortably on the edge of the bed, his hand clasping her mother's, his legs stretched to reach the floor.

They both looked so blissfully happy that Karen saw that her mother had forgotten her tiredness, and her father didn't know his legs were fast going to sleep.

She moved nearer, bending to kiss her mother. As she did so, she saw the tiny bundle which lay in Mary's arms.

As Karen watched, Mary drew back the shawl and the golden fuzz she had glimpsed became a soft covering of hair.

She watched in amazement as tiny fingers uncurled and soft pink lips opened in a huge yawn. In spite of herself she laughed, and the baby opened his eyes as if he heard her. Two bright blue eyes gazed up at her for a brief second before swimming out of focus.

"He looked at me!" Karen breathed. "Can he really see?"

"Not properly, but soon he'll be able to," her mother answered. "Soon he'll be a real person." She lifted the tiny bundle towards Karen.

"Put him back into his cot, love. I mustn't start spoiling him."

Karen took the surprisingly heavy bundle gingerly, scared she might hurt him.

"Hold him firmly," Mary warned her. "They soon know if you're scared, then they get frightened, too."

Karen tightened her grip, moving her baby brother into the curve of her arm. At the movement one of his hands pushed against the blanket and, as Karen touched the little fingers, they fastened round hers.

As she moved towards the cot something stirred inside her, and unthinkingly, her arms tightened around the baby. How could she have imagined she would hate this tiny scrap?

I NSTINCTIVELY she cradled his head as she laid him down in the cot and tucked the covers over him, and as she stepped back she saw the frills round the cot and the pink bows.

"Mum, pink bows! Did you want another girl?"

"We didn't really mind," Brian explained, and her mother laughed. "I don't suppose Edgar cares what colour the ribbons are. But that was the cot we had for you. I had to see what he was before I changed the bows.''

Karen looked from the bows to the baby sleeping peacefully beneath them, and her mother's words sank into her brain.

One day, over sixteen years ago, she must have lain in that same cot, and her mother and father had probably sat together just the way they were doing now.

Making sheep's eyes at each other, Karen thought, recalling Mrs Grant's description.

She looked over to her parents. It wasn't like that at all. That expression described something silly and fleeting, not the love which shone from her parents' faces.

This was love. The same sort of love she felt for Jeff.

Suddenly Karen saw how wrong she had been. It was love which had brought her into the world — she'd always accepted that. Why should it be so different now with Edgar? Just because her parents were older? Why should that make a difference?

This was the kind of love she'd hoped for, for her and Jeff. The kind that would last through the years.

With an abrupt movement Karen pushed her father's legs off the bed.

''Hey! Move over, make room for me. I remember we used to all fit in this bed at one time.''

She perched herself in the space where Brian's legs had crushed the covers, and took their hands.

''Now we're really a family,'' Karen declared, hoping they would understand what she was trying to tell them. She hadn't been jealous — well, maybe just a little — but now that was all over. Just as those other crazy notions had flown from her.

She gave their hands a little shake each as she went on.

''A proper family. You, Mum, me, Dad — and our Edgar.''

Her voice shook a little and she felt the tears threaten, but as the two sets of fingers gripped hers she knew that they had understood. Once again all was right with her world. □

W ILL that be all, then, Eleanor?'' Eleanor McCall hesitated for a
moment at the post office counter, then she smiled as Mrs Muir
counted up the stamps and postal orders she had bought.

"All for the post office, Mrs Muir, but I was wondering if you had
any of those pretty blue hair-combs left. The colour might match my
dress for the Hallowe'en Dance.''

Grace Muir smiled and moved over to a drawer behind the shop
counter, pulling out a cardboard box.

"One left, Eleanor. You'll be the belle of the ball, dear, as usual.''

Eleanor blushed and quickly paid her bill. People were always teasing
her about her looks, but she often felt she'd swap her golden hair and

peachy-soft complexion any day for the brains and competence of Mrs Muir's only daughter, Georgina.

They had been friends ever since they had been at school, but while Eleanor had settled down to helping her parents in their nursery, Georgina had qualified as a teacher and had gone to teach in one of the London schools.

"How is Georgina, Mrs Muir?" she asked shyly, with a trace of anxiety in her voice.

"Oh, she's doing well, but you'll see her for yourself soon. She's coming home on the twenty-eighth. In fact, she'll likely be going to the Hallowe'en Dance herself."

"Oh, that's lovely," Eleanor said, picking up her small package. "Cheerio then, Mrs Muir."

Eleanor's delicately-coloured cheeks were even more rosy as she walked home to Whitehills Nurseries. Christopher Fleming, who taught mathematics at the local comprehensive school, had already asked her to go to the dance with him, and Eleanor had accepted joyfully.

At first he'd just been another friend, but as she began to recognise his worth as a person, and to appreciate the depth to his character, Eleanor had fallen in love with Chris, and had long hoped that he would feel the same way about her.

She knew that he admired her looks and she'd often caught a light in

The Right One For Chris

By Jean Melville

his eyes when he came to pick her up for an evening's entertainment, and she had taken special pains over her appearance.

"Oh, Eleanor," he often said, tucking her hand into the crook of his arm, "I wonder if you realise how lovely you are. Where did you get that colour of hair?"

"From my mother," Eleanor would reply simply.

Mrs McCall's hair was now silver instead of gold, and her plump, energetic body was rather different from the slender one of her wedding photographs.

Sometimes Eleanor's eyes clouded when she looked at her mother. Mrs McCall was sweet and motherly, and Eleanor loved her very much, but her glowing beauty had not lasted. Perhaps it would not last with her either, Eleanor thought.

Wouldn't it be better to have a personality like Georgina's, she wondered. That could only grow with the years, and become even more interesting. And wouldn't Chris need that sort of personality for companionship rather than her own?

E LEANOR'S mind went back to the Hallowe'en Dance last year when all three of them had enjoyed the evening so very much.

She and Georgina had gone together, and Chris had danced with both of them.

"Are you both free on November the fifth?" he'd asked them.

"I'm supervising a bonfire party for the Cubs," he'd explained. "Why don't you come along and help? It should be good fun."

"I'd enjoy that," Eleanor had said eagerly. "I'll make some bonfire toffee for the boys, and my mother loves to make parkin."

"Splendid," Chris had said, "so long as you consider me 'one of the boys.' I can eat toffee with the best of them. That's settled, then."

"Well . . ." Georgina had hesitated, then she too capitulated. "Oh, all right, I'll come. I'm still getting used to supervising children. It's good practice."

For a while Eleanor had felt slightly left out as Chris and Georgina compared notes over their teaching activities, then Chris had turned to her with a smile.

"Were we talking shop, Eleanor?" he'd asked. "Sorry about that. Oh, it's the Dashing White Sergeant. Come on, girls, this is for us."

The Guy Fawkes party had been one which Eleanor would never forget. The boys were very excited, and the huge bonfire reflected the happy, laughing faces of the children who had all gathered together.

Chris set off the fireworks, while Eleanor handed round toffee and parkin. Only Georgina had appeared to be a trifle bored, and stood back on the outskirts of the crowd.

There wasn't a great deal to interest her, Eleanor thought, as she watched her friend sauntering about, her hands in the pockets of her duffel coat. Her dark hair was drawn into a bun at the nape of her neck, and in the firelight her pale face shone like a moonbeam. Georgina had her own type of beauty.

Suddenly one of the boys cried out in alarm as a lit match fell into a box of fireworks. Eleanor froze, aware of the danger, and, before she could say or do anything, Georgina had rushed past her and thrown her duffel coat on to the box, extinguishing the match!

It was all over in seconds and had been done with such speed and precision that Eleanor and Chris were left gasping. Chris recovered quickly enough to give the boys a severe lecture, then he turned to Georgina.

"I don't know how to say it," he said simply, "but thanks."

Eleanor had been full of admiration for her friend. It wasn't the first time that Georgina had reacted quickly in just such an emergency. She had once allowed a chip pan to go on fire when they were young teenagers, and Georgina had thrown a heavy towel over it. Mrs Muir had often said that her daughter was "very quick."

SHORTLY after the bonfire party, Georgina had gone back to London and had made brief visits home at Christmas and Easter.

During the long holidays, she'd helped her mother in the post office, and it was then that Eleanor had realised that she might be making a mistake in losing her heart to Chris Fleming.

She had often seen him and Georgina laughing together, and they appeared to have so much in common. They were really much more suited to one another, Eleanor thought, despondently, than she was to Chris.

And now the Hallowe'en Dance was coming round again, and Georgina would be home from London. Eleanor lifted her new dress out of the wardrobe, and held it up against herself.

It looked lovely, and she knew that she would have nothing to fear as far as her appearance was concerned. But was beauty enough? she wondered, afresh.

When Chris called to take her to the dance, Eleanor came downstairs wearing her new blue dress and hair ornament, a warm woollen shawl over her arm. The light from a chandelier lit up her hair and Chris walked forward, his eyes warm with appreciation. Mr and Mrs McCall had come out to see them away.

"I feel like the poor woodcutter taking out the princess," exclaimed Chris, as they drove away from the house.

"Oh, Chris, it isn't like that at all," Eleanor said, sighing a little. "Did you know that Georgina is home?"

"Yes, her mother mentioned it," he told her. "She likes this half-term holiday, I think. Eleanor . . . can we talk a little before we go to the dance?"

Chris had stopped the car, and had turned to look at the girl beside him. It was a clear moonlit night, and her lovely face was like a flower turned towards him.

"I . . . I feel that I've got rather a nerve proposing to you, Eleanor," he said. "I mean . . . I'm not exactly Prince Charming, while you . . . well . . . you're rather special when it comes to looks, but I do love you, darling, and I would try to make you happy."

Eleanor's heart bounded, then she bit her lip. At one time she would

D

have thrown her arms round Chris's neck, and accepted him on the spot, but over the past day or two she had done a lot of thinking.

She wasn't jealous of Georgina, but she had to acknowledge that there were girls like Georgina around who might be attractive to Chris one day — one day when her own looks had gone for ever. She wouldn't have much to offer Chris then.

"I want to marry you," he was saying. Slowly she pulled away from him.

"I . . . I don't know, Chris," she said unhappily.

FOR a long moment she could sense the stillness and disappointment in him.

"I love you, Chris," she said simply, and saw his face light up. "But I don't think I'm the right wife for you."

"Not the right wife!" he cried. "You're all the wife I want."

"But . . . Georgina . . . someone like Georgina is more for you, Chris."

"Georgina's a good friend, but she and I could never love one another," he said. "Whatever are you talking about?"

"I said someone *like* Georgina," she went on. "Please let me try to explain, Chris. I mean, looks don't last, especially my kind of looks. And . . . well . . . that's all I've got really. I'm not thinking of now, I'm thinking of twenty years from now. Just look at Georgina's mind compared with mine. Just remember last bonfire night, and how quickly she averted a serious accident to those fireworks.

"In a crisis I was absolutely helpless. It took her quick mind to sort it out. Her mind has been trained, just as yours has and you want someone who can match up to yourself, Chris, not me . . ."

Chris was silent for a while, then he shook his head slowly.

"You've thought about this a lot, haven't you?" he asked.

"Yes, I have."

"Then, doesn't that tell you something?" he asked gently. "When I say I love you, Eleanor, I mean I love all of you, not just your looks, though you'll still look beautiful to me when you're ninety. Don't you think that I love your honest mind, which pursues and works out problems, even if you aren't quite so quick as Georgina over some things.

"She is very good in a crisis, but I don't want to live all my life in a state of crisis, darling. I want all the lovely days when I have you to love, and your good sound commonsense to admire. And now you've taken the trouble to look ahead to the future, and tried to assess the years ahead, I can only marvel at your wisdom."

Chris was silent for a moment as he stroked her slender fingers.

"It frightens me a little, though. *You* could easily get fed up with an ordinary chap like me!"

"Not a chance!" Eleanor said, her happiness bubbling forth in laughter.

"Are we engaged then?" Chris asked.

"We're engaged," she agreed. □

The Place Where I Belong

By Phyllis Heath

TORONTO air terminal was crowded and John Davidson stood impatiently in the long line at the ticket desk. He had meant to arrive earlier, but he hadn't reckoned on being caught in the city's rush-hour traffic. He had also had several last-minute arrangements to make in order to be free to catch this flight, which was earlier than the one he'd intended taking.

Standing inches taller than the majority of his fellow passengers, he scanned those ahead searching for the long, wavy hair he remembered.

"I'd like you to look her up," Ronald Sinclair, the girl's father, had said, adding with the small town inhabitant's lack of comprehension of the size of Canada, "Rowena works in Toronto. I'll give you her address and so on."

John had nodded, not really meaning to do anything about it. But as the weeks of his stay passed he began to feel lonely, and he began to miss the lilting Scottish accent of his own people.

The scrap of paper Ronald had thrust into his hand bore a scribbled address and phone number. But it was nearly fifteen years since he'd last seen her. What if she didn't remember him? He would feel such a fool if he rang up and she didn't know him.

*   *   *   *

Rowena Sinclair felt the slight tug of her seat belt as the Jumbo jet lumbered up into the air and she turned to look out of the window.

51

As the plane circled, she looked down on the vast city, its streets laid out in straight, orderly lines. It was evening, but already the sky was black and the city lights glowed like a child's mosaic pattern; those scatterings of coloured balls she remembered from her childhood.

Her sigh of nostalgia caught the attention of the man sitting beside her.

"It's beautiful, isn't it? Indescribable," he commented.

Rowena smiled.

"I was just thinking it's like a child's mosaic."

The man's eyebrows rose and her face gleamed with mischief.

"Of course, you wouldn't know about such things, not unless you had sisters?" she continued.

"Unfortunately not."

"Well, when I was a little girl my father bought me a box of metallic coloured beads. There was a black board with holes and you made patterns with the balls. And it looked just like that." She gestured back to the receding view.

"I don't think I've ever seen one of those things, but I can imagine exactly what you mean."

His tone was admiring and Rowena felt bound to explain.

"Colour and design is my work. It's natural for me to see things that way." She dropped her voice hesitantly and turned back to the window, though there was nothing to see but the night sky and her own reflection.

What on earth had made her say all that? In fact, what had made her talk to this stranger in the first place?

John fell silent, too, the moment lost.

Why hadn't he spoken? It would have been so simple to say, "Don't I know you?" No, that was too pat, too obviously a line. "Haven't we met before?" — no, that sounded even worse!

John shifted restlessly in his seat. All that explaining to her flatmate, when he'd finally plucked up courage to call, only to discover she was returning to Scotland that very day.

After that there'd been a mad dash to the airport, followed by several frantic phone calls to people he wouldn't be able to see when he'd discovered he could change his flight to be on the same plane as Rowena.

And now he had to go and behave like a stupid schoolboy!

It was her looks which had thrown him. Ronald Sinclair hadn't told him she was beautiful. He wasn't used to beautiful, assured, young women who spoke with a delightful Canadian-Scottish accent.

John was glad when the hostess came to take orders for drinks.

Rowena was pleased that the man beside her didn't offer to buy her anything. The omission allowed her to relax.

D O you fly often?" John Davidson asked, when they'd been served.

"Not this route."

"But you *are* Scottish, aren't you?"

She couldn't help laughing.

"According to the Canadians there's no doubt — but actually I've lived in Toronto for years. I'm on a visit home."

"And you wish you weren't," he said and Rowena flushed at his perception.

"My father lives in a tiny village. He's had a heart attack," she explained.

"I'm sorry."

"Thanks, but apparently he's not too bad." Rowena fell silent. She had only had her aunt's short cable, she hadn't waited for a letter. And even though Aunt Catherine hadn't sounded as if she expected her home, she'd decided to make the trip all the same.

I suppose I did shake the dust of Scotland off my feet pretty rapidly, Rowena thought. But I felt stifled there.

A smile touched her lips — how absurd that sounded! Stifled, in a land of moors and lochs, and acres and acres of nothing but scenery.

But it described how she'd felt, ever since she'd discovered that there was a whole world just waiting to be found, somewhere out there, beyond the mountains.

When her training as a fashion buyer gave her the opportunity and the excuse, she had spread her wings and flown. First to Edinburgh, then to London, and finally to Toronto.

TEXAS had a reputation for being bigger and better than anywhere else in the world, but for Rowena this applied to Canada.

And now she was going back to Scotland!

"And you? I guess you're not Canadian?" Rowena said pleasantly.

"No fear!" John Davidson laughed. "Not that I didn't enjoy my visit," he added hastily.

"What did you see? The Falls?"

"Of course!" He grinned. "But I can see plenty of water back home. It was the forests I went to see."

Rowena turned to look at him in surprise.

"Trees are my business, just as colour is yours. My, they certainly have a lot of timber over there."

She looked at his big, square hands and the breadth of his shoulders. She could just imagine him in a check shirt and jeans, wielding a large axe.

"But you're glad to be going back?" she asked.

"All those people and buildings! Ay! I liked it fine, for a visit, but it's not my kind of place. They've some grand country — the forests, as I said, and the rivers. But it's so big! You have to travel miles before there's a change of scenery. In Scotland there's a surprise round every wee corner."

His accent had grown progressively thicker as he talked and Rowena realised why there had been a vague feeling of familiarity about him.

"You sound just like my father!" she exclaimed and was glad when he misunderstood her.

"He likes Scotland then."

She nodded, then turning away, stared pensively out of the window.

"So he won't want to leave. Isn't there anyone who could take care of him?" John asked.

"There's his sister, Aunt Catherine. But she lives down in England. I don't know whether he'd be fit enough . . ."

Her voice tailed away. It wasn't just her father's health which would be the stumbling block. What if he wouldn't move? She couldn't just desert him. He might not be well enough to live alone.

John Davidson watched the emotions cross her face.

"It'll be hard," he agreed. "But, you don't know yet. He might be well enough to go home, to be by himself. You don't know. I shouldn't worry until it's time to worry."

"No," Rowena said. "You're right, of course."

She tried to put the matter behind her and concentrate on the tales John was telling her about his trip, but though he was an excellent raconteur she was glad when their meal was served, and he turned his attention to that.

Later she slept, and wakened to find the dawn turning the edges of the wings to fire. She heard John's gasp of astonished delight beside her.

"For a moment I thought something was wrong. I couldn't believe what I was seeing. That's some sight!" he said in amazement.

She was amused by his almost childlike delight in the scene.

"I've seen the sun come up across a loch, or high among the hills, but I'm not sure that doesn't beat everything," he went on quietly.

He made her feel blase and jaded.

> ## Commuters
>
> IS it just imagination
>   Makes me think you glance my way?
> Makes me wonder, if you should speak,
>   Just what things you'd choose to say.
> Eyes reflected in the window
>   Follow every move I make,
> Or is it just foolish fancy?
>   Have I made a big mistake?
> Jolting . . . halting at a station.
>   Jostling travellers make us touch.
> Moments till our destination,
>   Little time to learn so much.
> Shyly I discuss the weather,
>   In the clatter miss your name,
> But I hear the words that matter,
>   "See you on the evening train!"
>   *Sylvia Hart.*

"It's a grand sight," he repeated as the sky lit up before them, turning from red to pink.

Rowena turned towards him, wanting to share his enjoyment, but the admiration she saw in his eyes made her turn quickly away again, the pink colour touching her face until she was as flushed as the dawn sky.

"We're coming over land," she told him, keeping her gaze fixed on the scene below.

John leaned over, peering at the faint coastline, and his arm brushed hers, his face close, so that his breath lifted the strands of her hair which had worked loose during the night.

Rowena drew back in her seat, her heart missing a beat.

This was ridiculous! What was there about this man to disturb her natural calm?

She looked round the dimly-lit cabin, where people spoke in whispers and the rising sun tinged the tiny windows with gold.

Who wouldn't be affected in such an atmosphere? The man beside her was attractive, there was no denying it. Not only that but he seemed kind, gentle; a direct contrast from the rather brash, confident, young men she had grown used to.

But I like Canadian men! I don't want to become involved with anyone from "back home." Ships that pass in the night, she reminded herself. I'll probably never see him again.

S TANDING at the baggage carousel, feeling in need of a shower and a long sleep, Rowena heard John's voice beside her.

"How are you getting to town? My car's parked nearby if you'd like a lift."

"Oh, I couldn't!" Rowena shot round, her eyes wide with dismay. John smiled.

"It's all right. I won't kidnap you. Those sort of things don't happen in dozy Scotland."

She didn't remember accepting his offer but soon she was sitting beside him, the countryside spinning by.

"Now you must admit it is beautiful!" he said.

"I didn't say it wasn't. That's what I'm afraid of."

"Afraid?"

"I don't want it to get a hold of me again. My life's in Canada. My work's there, my home," she replied emphatically.

John heard the passion in her voice and chuckled.

"There's no need to be quite so assertive. Who are you trying to convince?"

After that there seemed little to talk about, but, as the outskirts of the city drew near, John asked, "The hospital? Is your father in the General? I could take you there."

"But it's 'way out the other side of town."

"I know. You forget I'm from round these parts." He swung the car away from the town centre and, when they reached the hospital, he ignored her proffered hand.

"I'll come in with you. I won't be in the way, but . . ." He shrugged as fear showed in her eyes. "Your father will be all right, don't worry. You'd have heard if there'd been any change."

When she arrived in the ward, Ronald Sinclair was sitting propped up against a mound of pillows.

"You're early. I've only just had my breakfast," he greeted her, and she laughed at his brusqueness, sensing the affection underneath.

"Really, Dad, anyone would think you weren't pleased to see me," she teased.

"No more I am. Your Aunt Catherine shouldn't have sent for you. But you know your aunt," he answered testily.

"I know you, too," she rejoined. "Stubborn old man. And I didn't come straight from the airport to get into bother, or to waste the few minutes Sister's given us arguing."

"It's good to have you back. I don't know when I last enjoyed a conversation so much." Ronald grinned.

"I got a lift from the airport, from a man who lives in the neighbourhood. I was sitting next to him on the plane and he wouldn't take no for an answer. I must be losing my touch. He's outside. A Mr John Davidson."

"I'm not surprised you couldn't get rid of him, not John Davidson. Don't you remember him?" her father asked.

Rowena pondered.

"I don't think so, though now you come to mention it, there was something vaguely familiar about him."

"Of course you know him. But, I'm forgetting. You were only children and you'd have known him as Jackie Burns."

He watched enlightenment dawn in Rowena's face.

"Jackie Burns! But why Davidson?"

Her mind pictured the tousle-haired boy who had never been happy unless he was fishing or tramping over the hills. Yes, it fitted.

"The Burns weren't his parents — John was orphaned. But I suppose you children never bothered with such niceties. The people he lived with were called Burns and so was he," Ronald explained.

Rowena nodded. It certainly explained the faint familiarity and her inability to place John.

"Bring him in," Ronald demanded. "I'd like to have a crack with wee Jackie."

JOHN drove her home. This time she didn't protest except to ask why he hadn't told her who he was.

He glanced momentarily from the road, his eyes dancing with mischief.

"Would it have made you more friendly to the country boy? If so, I wish I had told you."

"You haven't changed," she told him. "I remember you used to chase us with snails and long, fat worms. Horrid child you were."

But when her aunt greeted John just as effusively as her father had, Rowena felt piqued. An emotion which was reinforced by the way the villagers smiled and chatted with him.

"I feel I'm a stranger around here. They all ask when I'm going back. This is my home, too, you know!" Rowena complained.

John often drove her into the hospital, until there was no more need for daily visits. Then he took her out among the hills he loved.

She rediscovered the places of her childhood — the streams running crystal clear over the stony bottoms, the springy bracken, the rough bark of trees, and everywhere the pleasant, tangy smell she couldn't define.

"It's fresh air," John told her. "You've forgotten what it smells like. I don't know how you live breathing that stuff which passes for oxygen out there."

Rowena didn't speak. It was a conspiracy. Everyone seemed to be trying to bring her back.

The Place Where I Belong

THEY had been resting after their long climb from the valley. John stretched full length, his eyes closed, his breathing so even that she had fancied he was asleep.

She had sat, her legs drawn up to her body, her arms wrapped round them, her chin on her hands, gazing down on to the village where her father lived.

Everything was so still and quiet. Seeing the grey stone building, which she knew was the old school, she remembered a poem she had learned there.

Dear God, the very houses seem asleep.

The poet hadn't been writing about this, or any village, but he might have been.

"It is asleep. They're all asleep. It's all so quiet!" she said angrily.

John opened one eye and looked up at her.

"Lovely, isn't it?"

"Of course it's lovely. No-one in their right mind would deny that. But it's not for me. So why do you all feel I must worship it, too?" she demanded.

John sat up but he didn't answer. He seemed to know she didn't expect an answer.

"That's what you've been doing, isn't it? All the weeks I've been here. You've been setting the countryside before me as if it was your own private possession — your own paradise."

Still he didn't speak.

"The people — you've been putting them on show, too. Their friendliness, their kindness, everything! But it isn't enough. Of course, I love this place. But it isn't enough. I won't stay. I won't!"

John rose to his feet, staring into the valley, avoiding her furious eyes.

"Yes, I wanted you to come to love this place. Not only because I think it's beautiful, but partly because I think you'd be losing something if you leave without knowing what you're missing. That was the way I started out, Rowena. But it's changed."

Rowena held her breath, knowing what was coming but unable to prevent him saying it.

"I love you, Rowena. I want you to stay. I want to . . ." He broke off as Rowena covered her ears.

"Don't say it. Don't! I worked and slaved for the life I've made. I can't stay."

She turned to look at him and saw the sorrow in his eyes, and her voice softened.

"I'm sorry, John. It wouldn't work. You love it here, the peace, the solitude, *your* forests, as you call them."

"But they *are* mine," he said.

"But not mine! I don't want them. I don't want any part of them, or the village, or the peace. I'm going home, John."

She picked up her bag and began to stride down the hill and John followed her, his eyes dark with pain.

That evening she rang the airline and booked her flight.

"There's been a cancellation. I can fly Saturday," she told her father.

R OWENA carried her cases down into the narrow hallway and kissed her aunt, hugging her father fiercely.

"Look after yourself. I'll be back on a visit. Maybe you could come out there to see me."

"Maybe." Ronald Sinclair didn't sound very sure.

John drove her to the airport.

"We'll miss you," was all he said, but his face looked so blank she stayed with him until it was almost time for her flight.

When the speakers called her flight number, she took his hands, standing with arms outstretched, out of his reach.

"Goodbye, John. Goodbye." Swiftly she kissed him, tearing her hands from his, feeling the rough skin of his hands rasp against hers, bringing its own particular pain.

Then she ran, following the last group of passengers, her fingers still tingling from the force of John's grasp.

Before she passed out of the lounge she looked back. Back through the tunnel of people which surged into the gap she had left. Back to where John was standing.

And as John's eyes sought hers she recognised the pain she was feeling for what it was. Slowly she began to walk back to him.

When she stood close, she looked up at him.

"I don't know what we're going to do about these." She thrust out her ticket and boarding card. "You've won. I'm not going back. I'm staying here." Her tone was belligerent.

"Darling Rowena. I've been wishing and praying, praying and wishing. I thought I'd lost you. You were right. I was trying to get you under the spell of this country. And it worked. Glory be! It worked," John cried happily.

He was laughing, saying her name and kissing her in turn, and Rowena began to laugh, too.

"No! No, it didn't work, John. It's not the place I love. It isn't your sparkling burns or your heather-covered hills. I don't love the place now any more than I did before. It's you, you fool! It's you I love."

Again he kissed her and overhead the Tannoy call for her.

"Shut up," Rowena ordered it. "Shut up, can't you? This is where I belong," she told the speaker, snuggling deeper into John's arms. "This is where I belong." □

Perhaps one of the finest lochs in Scotland, Loch Maree is about 12½ miles long and one to three miles broad. Presiding majestically over the loch is Slioch, 3217 feet high. One of the many islets that dot the loch's waters is tiny Isle Maree, where Druids once worshipped. On the isle are the ruins of a chapel founded by St Maelrubha. Nearby is a sacred well. Set among the wild mountain scenery there can be few more impressive and changeless sights.

LOCH MAREE : J CAMPBELL KERR

Picture Of Happiness

A WREN fluttered noisily on to the window sill. Ella Logan paused to watch its antics, smiling a little as she stood at her easel, letting her brush rest against her colourful palette.

Then, she gradually became aware of a distinct aroma of roast beef and she gave an exclamation of dismay. Hastily wiping her hands on a rag, she hurried out of her cluttered studio.

She ought never to have started painting, she thought with a pang of conscience — not when her daughter Ivy was bringing a boyfriend to Sunday tea. And she'd promised Ivy that everything would be perfect too.

In the kitchen, fortunately, Ken Logan was obviously very much in charge. He gave his wife a smile of reassurance and told her that the meal was under control.

"I'm so sorry," Ella ran a distracted hand through her dark hair, "I only went into the studio for a moment." She rubbed her aching wrists. "I'd no intention of working for hours."

Again Ken smiled at her, a tolerant, relaxed smile.

"You know I enjoy cooking," he said. "So Ivy's portrait will be finished, is it?"

Ella shook her head, frowning.

"No, I can't see myself ever finishing that one, I'm afraid. I looked at it yesterday and it's just not Ivy at all. There's an air of gloom all about it, her whole face seems to be drooping."

She sighed despondently. Then her expression brightened.

"It was Jenny Watson's picture I was trying to finish. She posed for me last week on the wooden bridge beside the burn. And today, when I went to take a peek at what I'd done so far, I was so pleased that I had one of these 'did I do that?' sensations — and then, well you know what happened, I got carried away!"

Ken put down the dish he was holding and came across to put his hands on her shoulders.

"I suppose I ought to tell you you look lovely when your hair's standing on end and your face is streaked with paint." He paused, and planted a kiss on her nose. "But you don't, you know. If Ivy arrives with this perfect gentleman of hers, she'll be positively ashamed of her mother."

Ella summoned up a strained smile.

"Do you think it's going to be awful? I've warned the boys to behave and if the twins start giggling . . ."

"Stop worrying." Ken hugged her gently. "It'll only be worse if we're all on edge."

"Yes, I expect you're right," she said, adding, "I'll come back and help you after I've cleaned my brushes."

By
Peggy Maitland

"And yourself!" he reminded her, as she moved towards the door, and as she opened it he called, "How many are we for tea, by the way? Is Ewan coming?"

She nodded, sighing.

"I said he needn't if he didn't want to. But he said Ivy had specially asked him to come as usual. I don't think she realises that Ewan . . ." She paused and shrugged helplessly, adding, "Maybe she wants him to help us to mind our manners. But I really thought he'd prefer to opt out."

"He probably thinks it's wiser to weigh up the opposition." Ken pulled a face. "Anyhow," he went on cheerfully, "that makes it eleven for tea. And talk of the devil!"

The back door opened and Ewan Ritchie came in carrying a large basket of vegetables.

Ella threw him only a brief greeting before she hurried out, leaving the two men together. She wondered what they'd be saying about the forthcoming meal and the presence of Ivy's boyfriend.

But neither man mentioned that subject. It wasn't Ken's way to agonise about something that couldn't be helped. And Ewan had decided, well in advance, that he must be cautious. Nothing must induce him to reveal the depths of his hurt.

THERE was no special understanding between Ewan and Ivy. Bitterness tinged his thoughts now as he chatted with Ivy's father about the garden and this year's bumper crop of vegetables. Maybe she still thinks of me as the boy who does the garden to earn some pocket money, he mused.

Once that had been the case. He'd been glad enough of any odd jobs while he was a schoolboy, keen to help the family budget when his father's business had struck a bad patch.

When Mrs Logan had asked him in for the odd meal, he'd accepted eagerly, in the hope that he would get to know Ivy better. And of course that had inevitably happened.

In recent years, though, his Sunday work in the garden had been more in the nature of a favour to his friends. Now he was working in his father's builders' yard, but he still loved the Logans' garden, and best of all, the Sunday teas — only last week, Ivy had reminded him that he was her best friend, as they strolled in the garden in the evening.

When she'd told him that she planned to invite George Forsyth to tea, Ewan's immediate reaction had been to say that he would give the garden a miss, for once.

"But I'm depending on you, Ewan," she'd pleaded, her eyes wide and appealing. "You can always keep the boys from squabbling and the twins behave much better when you're around. They try to impress you. You're their hero."

Very conscious of the blush he couldn't control, Ewan was completely tongue-tied. Much as he longed to speak of the love which throbbed in his heart, he just couldn't seem to frame the correct words. And in the end, Ivy had persuaded him that his help was vital to her.

"It's not that I'm ashamed of my family and my home," Ivy had said, "I love them dearly . . . but the whole household's so unmanageable, so chaotic. My mother's a great person and quite good looking when she isn't covered in paint. And my father's wonderful with animals. Do you think if he'd been a schoolteacher instead of a vet, we'd have been a more normal family?"

"There's nothing wrong with your family — I like them," Ewan had answered, shrugging uncomfortably.

But there was to be no contradicting Ivy.

"And neither of them seem to bother about Granny and Aunt Kate filling every inch of space in the house with junk that they call antiques!" she'd continued. "Maybe it's just as well that one or other of my brothers can guarantee to break something at least once a day." She'd looked at him distractedly.

"Did you know that the cat got stuck inside that Chinese urn last week? Granny cried and said that if the cat starved for a day or two it would soon get out. But Rob smashed the urn anyhow," and, as her eyes filled with tears, she'd said, "I couldn't bear it if anything like that happens while George is here."

Ewan had tried to reassure her. But now, as he heard the sound of a car outside, he had grave misgivings about the guest's ability to cope with the boisterous, rather eccentric Logans.

A LREADY the sixteen-year-old twins, Rose and Rita, could be heard giggling as they clumped downstairs. And the boys, twelve-year-old Douglas and ten-year-old Rob, had evidently sighted the car and were expressing their opinion of it in loud voices.

Outside, Ivy was getting out of the car and trying to smile serenely as she reproved the boys. But it was hopeless trying to introduce them to George. They were already walking round the car, admiringly, approvingly, demanding to know what mileage it had done and how many miles to the gallon it did.

George was flattered by their interest and did his best to answer all the questions they were firing at him. But Ivy could see that he was slightly overwhelmed and after a moment, she rescued him by linking her arm through his and drawing him firmly towards the front door.

She'd told him all their names, of course, and described the family as best she could, glossing over their little foibles and faults. She'd warned him about the dogs, too, telling him that all three of them were inclined to be extra affectionate when they wanted to make friends with anyone new.

And sure enough, the dogs came hurtling from nowhere to hurl themselves with abandon at the newcomer as they entered the house. But George didn't seem to mind at all. Ivy was proud of him as she made all the introductions amidst a background of laughing struggles with the excited dogs.

Eventually, the dogs were banished to the garden and Mrs Logan suggested that everyone should go straight into the dining-room as the meal was ready.

As they all trooped obediently in, Ivy could not suppress a renewed flutter of apprehension, as she visualised some unforeseen catastrophe — or worse — utter silence!

Before they were even settled in their places, Ivy heard her grandmother beginning to question George, asking him what he did for a living.

Ivy's heart sank. Her grandmother knew very well that he was a sales manager in the company she worked for. She recalled the wry face that Granny had made when she'd boasted that George was the youngest ever sales manager. Was she planning to take George down a peg if he told her anything like that?

But George wasn't telling the old woman about his success in business, nor was he evading her searching questions. He simply made his work sound rather boring and unimportant and adroitly turned the conversation to her own favourite pastime — buying antiques from auction sales around the country.

When she heard her grandmother launching into a long anecdote about a chair she'd bought and restored and sold again, Ivy began to relax. Catching her mother's eye, she gave a small smile.

Ella Logan smiled back at her daughter, making a slight movement of her head to indicate that she approved of the young man from the city. Then she glanced at her husband, who conveyed a signal that he shared her opinion.

As the evening progressed it was clearly evident that they all liked George. His modest, unassuming amiability seemed to blend very well with the family's willingness to accept him into their circle.

A ROUND nine o'clock, Ivy went to the kitchen with her mother to help to prepare a snack supper.

"Well, I'd say the ice is well and truly broken now," Mrs Logan remarked. "You'll be able to bring George back without getting into a panic next time — don't you think?"

Ivy nodded.

"Was I dreadful, Mum?" she asked penitently. "I can't believe I criticised you all . . . and made everyone promise to behave. It was terrible of me, wasn't it?"

"Not at all," Ella Logan answered briskly, "I expect it was good for us to be drilled up a bit. We're far too slap-dash."

"No, Mum, that's not true," Ivy interrupted, and giving her mother a swift spontaneously affectionate hug, "I wouldn't want you to be any different — I wouldn't change you for the world!"

Her mother kissed her cheek.

"I know that, Ivy — I understand how you felt about today," she said tenderly.

They moved away from each other as the sound of voices from the garden drifted in through the open window.

"The menfolk are surely taking the air," Mrs Logan said lightly, but as she and Ivy continued to put sandwiches and cake and biscuits on plates, the mood of tender closeness stayed with them, and Mrs Logan found herself telling Ivy how much they all missed her while she was away working in the city.

It was the first time her mother had said such a thing, although Ivy had been away for almost four months.

"I'm starting to miss you, too," Ivy confessed. "Everything was a novelty at first. There wasn't time to be homesick — and then I started going out with George . . ."

Her voice faltered and tailed off. She was pensive for a long moment before she went on.

"I'll be off next Monday — perhaps I'll come home for a long weekend."

"I'll look forward to that," Mrs Logan said happily, and after a slight pause, she added, "and I don't have to tell you that George would be welcome — if you want to bring him."

"I'm not sure," Ivy replied vaguely. "I'll ring you during the week."

Tactfully, Mrs Logan said no more. She could vaguely remember what it felt like to be hovering on the delicate, uncertain verge of falling in love. But even although she had no fault to find with George Forsyth, she couldn't help wishing that Ivy's choice had been Ewan, whose love for her amounted almost to adoration.

Outside in the garden, Mr Logan had stopped to light his pipe while George and Ewan walked on towards the rose garden.

OVERHEARD ON A TRAIN

*S*AID *a lady to her companions –*
"One time I was in London by myself. Bought what I came for – much else too.

"Well, on the train home to Aberdeen, dinner was called and me starving. So I made for the dining-car; checked my purse at the door. Only some silver! All I had left.

"I stood there numb – the aroma of food so strong.

" 'Coming in?' asked the attendant – I knew he was an Aberdonian by his voice.

" 'I wish I could but I can't,' and told him my plight. Know what he did? Takes out his wallet and hands me, a total stranger, £10. I was overcome!

"How was he sure I could be trusted to pay him back," I asked him.

" 'Because,' said she, 'ye've a guid honest North face upon ye!' "

Rev. T. R. S. Campbell.

Lingering all week at the back of Ewan's mind there had been a vague notion of saying something, anything to spoil the blossoming romance between George and Ivy. But now that he had an ideal opportunity, he did not even try. He could not bring himself to betray Ivy's trust.

George offered him a cigarette. But he refused, saying that he didn't smoke, he'd never started.

"It's a bad habit," George agreed, adding with a grin, "I've only had one all afternoon, though I was practically chain smoking on the way here, I felt so nervous about whether Ivy's family would accept me."

Ewan felt quite touched by the other man's very frank admission.

"You needn't have worried," he said kindly. "Ivy's family are the same as she is."

George nodded his agreement.

"Yes, they're all marvellous people." And as one of the dogs came running towards them, he added in supremely victorious tones, "Even the dogs seem to have taken to me."

Country bumpkin me, Ewan raged at himself later. Why did I have to be pleasant to him? Couldn't I have at least found a way to let him know that I have a claim on Ivy too?

I T wasn't until the following Friday evening that he saw Ivy again. She was walking towards the village hall.

"I thought I might as well look in on the dance," she said, crossing the road to lean on the wall of the builder's yard where he was working late.

For a moment he was speechless. Then he tossed away the paving slab he was holding.

"Wait for me then! Come on, into the house — I'll be ready in five minutes!" he cried eagerly.

In the shower, he could hardly keep from singing. He knew Ivy! He could tell from her expression, from the look in her eyes, that everything was over between her and George. This time I'll make sure I don't miss my chance, he determined. This very night I'll tell her I love her and ask her to marry me.

But on the way home from the dance, when he took Ivy in his arms, she moved her lips away from his passionate kiss. And when he tried to tell her that he loved her she put her finger on his lips.

"Don't say that, Ewan." Her voice was sad and resigned. "I don't want you to say that. You see, I've decided that I'm too young to get involved in a close relationship."

Ewan frowned, almost stunned by her reaction.

"But I thought when I saw you alone earlier on that you'd come to your senses about that other fellow!" he exclaimed.

She moved out of his arms, and they began to walk on slowly.

"I really thought I was in love with George," she sighed, "and maybe I still am. I'm just not sure . . . He wants us to get engaged . . . but I've told him I'm too young."

"Ivy, if you love somebody there aren't any doubts," he said in a choked voice. "And age has nothing to do with it. I've loved you since we were children — only I was too shy to say so. And then last Sunday I was incredibly stupid . . ." He bit his lip, afraid he'd said too much.

"Stupid? How do you mean?" She tried to see his face in the darkness, as she told him, "I always think of you as being very wise."

Softly, regretfully, he recounted his conversation with George Forsyth, and his subsequent thoughts.

"I suppose I virtually gave you up to him — because I thought it was him you wanted," he confessed.

"Did you do that for me?" Ivy asked in wondering tones.

"Ivy, I'd do anything in the world for you," Ewan said, and drawing her back into his arms, he added masterfully, "Anything, except let you go again!"

But by now they had reached the Logans' home, and as her twin sisters could be heard approaching with the boys who had walked them home, Ivy said a swift goodnight and slipped out of his arms.

Not wanting to to talk to anyone, she sped upstairs to her room, her mind racing with a turbulent mixture of questions and emotions. It seemed almost impossible to sort them all out. But before she fell asleep at last, she knew she'd found the answer to her dilemma.

N EXT day, the morning began with glorious sunshine. Mrs Logan couldn't wait to get into her studio to paint. The light was absolutely perfect for finishing the landscape she had sketched yesterday.

But as she began to prepare the colours she would use, her eye was suddenly caught by the unfinished portrait of Ivy.

Critically, she studied it from all angles. No, it just wasn't Ivy . . . perhaps if she could just find a way to heighten the cheekbones, lift the corners of the mouth . . .

Ella Logan's mind began to work like lightning but her hands worked much more slowly as she altered the image on the canvas with infinite care.

It was some hours later when the studio door opened that she became conscious of the passage of time.

"Want some lunch?" Ken Logan asked. As she turned, he added apologetically, "I thought all the noise would have disturbed you anyhow, so I . . ." He stopped abruptly as his eyes came to rest on the portrait.

"Well, that's our girl!" He gave a long whistle.

His wife looked at her work appraisingly.

"It's much more like her," she said, delighted with the sparkling-eyed effect, the sheer joy in the laughing face.

"Did you guess? Or were you hoping?" Ken gave her a quizzical glance.

She threw him a puzzled look. But before she could ask a question, he called out to the rest of the family to come and look.

Then as they all began to crowd into the room, she saw at once that Ivy and Ewan were hand in hand. Ewan had the air of someone who would never let go.

Happily, Ella Logan listened to the chorus of admiring comments. Her heart was full and her eyes were misty with tears as she realised that some instinct had shown her how to anticipate Ivy's look of happiness.

"Seems to me you've been captured for life, Ivy, my girl," her grandmother commented and Ivy's laughter blended with Ewan's.

But Ewan had the last word.

"I hope you'll consider giving it to us for a wedding present, Mrs Logan." □

For Love Of Sheila

by Margaret Black

S TOP!'' The sudden exclamation from his companion made Keith
  Heriot brake the car sharply, so that the picnic bag fell off the back
  seat with a thud.

"What is it, Sheila?" He was alarmed.

"I saw a garden."

Keith drew in at the side of the road on the outskirts of the village
through which he had just driven and looked uncomprehendingly at the
girl beside him.

"A garden, Keith — a beautiful garden and a man working in it."

Keith's expression grew more dazed. Words failed him. He was beginning to realise just how often they failed him with Sheila, whom he was — or believed he was — eventually going to marry.

He had fallen in love with her when they met at a wedding, fallen in love in a way which he, twenty-seven years old and already doing very well as a quantity surveyor, had never imagined in his wildest dreams that he would.

His well-ordered life had been planned out. He'd already reached most of his goals and marriage was not one of them — not for years anyway — and then he'd met Sheila and in no time she'd managed to turn his well-ordered life on its head.

First of all, simply falling in love had driven his commonsense out of the window. Secondly, Sheila was as unpredictable as mercury.

At first he'd adored all the unexpected things about her — her vivid imagination, her lively sense of humour and her readiness to adopt any and every lame dog that crossed her path. He also loved her red hair, her smiling brown eyes, the dimple at the side of her mouth and her low, gurgling laugh.

He still loved all those things, but what had marked her as so delightfully different from all the other girls he'd previously met had of late started to become just very slightly exasperating.

He knew now that there would be a few things about Sheila he'd like to change. He still loved her but he no longer found her absolutely perfect.

So today he looked at her with exasperation and at the same time fought down the desire to kiss her, just where the dimple quirked the side of her mouth.

"Did I scare you, Keith? I didn't mean to. I just saw this man working in the garden and it was the oddest thing. Do let's go back and have another look."

"Not till you tell me more," Keith said firmly. "You're not making sense."

"Then you wait here and I'll go back myself." Sheila laughed, jumping out of the car in a flash of long, slim legs.

"Sheila . . ."

But she was gone and, grumbling, he switched off the engine and followed her. It was only fifty yards and he caught up with her before she reached the dilapidated garden gate.

SHEILA turned to him with the smile which usually melted his heart.
"See." She lowered her voice. "The garden's so well kept but there isn't a house, just that old ruin of a cottage sitting in the middle of it all."

She was right. The garden was a blaze of flowers and the well-weeded beds immaculate. The heady scent blew across to them in the afternoon breeze. The paths were neat and the borders tidy, but the roof of the cottage was off and it was the picture of neglect.

Ten yards away a man was hoeing. He was a broad-shouldered young man with fair hair glinting in the sun. The sleeves of his checked shirt were rolled up revealing a pair of muscular arms.

Sheila looked again at the ruin of a cottage and turned to her companion.

"It's fascinating, isn't it? I wonder why. I'll ask him."

"Don't . . ."

It was useless. Weeks ago he had realised he'd never stop Sheila talking to anyone and everyone. She had the friendliness of a young puppy, and he tended to find it slightly embarrassing, because he had a strain of well-hidden shyness in his own make-up, which he'd never admit, even to himself.

So he didn't follow Sheila but stood in the road, feeling extremely stupid, watching while the man stopped work and leaned on his hoe, while he and Sheila carried on an animated conversation.

"Keith," she called to him but he didn't join them. He did, however, move inside the gate feeling that this was enough of a gesture.

THE breeze was blowing Sheila's red hair across her brow and the sun was bright on it. It tugged, too, at her thin skirt so that it belled out, making her waist very tiny.

The conversation was lively and Keith watched what he couldn't hear. Surely Sheila didn't have to be so animated even although she was a keen gardener. She was looking up into the face of this perfect stranger and giving him the kind of smiles which Keith preferred to have directed at himself.

When Sheila finally came back to join him, she turned at the gate to wave and shout goodbye and the young man waved back, grinning broadly.

"You should have come over, Keith! He's such a nice fellow. His name's Alan Ramage."

"And I suppose you gave him your name, too — a perfect stranger!"

The sarcasm was lost on Sheila, who nodded blithely.

"It's most interesting about the cottage, Keith."

"Tell me about it in the car."

She told him, while he started the car and began driving along the country road. They were less than twenty miles from Glasgow, although it seemed more remote.

"The cottage belongs to an old great-aunt of his, who's permanently in hospital in Glasgow. She's promised to leave it to him so long as he keeps the garden just as she remembers it. She hasn't lived in it since she was a child and he had to start from scratch — a lot of work. He takes photographs to the hospital to show her."

"I never heard anything so silly!"

"Oh, Keith!" Sheila turned on him, obviously disappointed. "He hopes to renovate the cottage and live in it. He thinks she might give it to him quite soon now he has the garden in shape. He can't start on the cottage till it's actually his."

"If you want my opinion, I think the old lady's doing a fine spot of blackmail and the man's a fool, because he has no guarantee she won't change her mind and give it to someone else. I still think it's the silliest thing I ever heard of."

A silence fell. It lengthened until Keith took his eyes off the road long enough to glance at his companion. He saw there were tears in her eyes and he was immediately contrite.

"I'm sorry."

"It is a lovely story, isn't it, Keith — a beautiful garden but no house?" she said coaxingly.

He didn't even nod, but he remained silent, listening to her. He loved her. When he looked at her, his bones turned to water.

THEY had their picnic beside a river, sitting on a travelling rug. It was a beautiful day, the sun high and the clouds like white puff balls.

"Alan Ramage will be hot, working in the garden on a day like this," Sheila observed, biting into a sandwich.

By now, Keith had almost forgotten the man and the reminder was not welcome. It seemed as if one of those puff ball clouds had momentarily drifted across the sun.

He leaned up on his elbow.

"Forget Alan Ramage and think about us."

She was quite willing to do so and the rest of the day passed very pleasantly until he delivered her back at her home in the evening.

"Next Saturday I thought we could go to Aviemore, Sheila, unless you have another idea."

"Keith, one Saturday I'd really like to go back and see how the garden is getting on. It fascinates me. I'd love to know if Alan Ramage does get the house soon."

Keith closed his lips and carefully made no comment.

"Why the scowl? You look positively fierce. You can't — you simply can't be jealous of a garden!"

"I'm not jealous at all. You're being childish!"

It was the nearest they'd come to a quarrel and it cast quite a blight for several days. Keith was furious with himself and even more furious with the innocent cause of the trouble, the young man with the garden — Alan Ramage.

It was only too obvious Sheila was intrigued by the story of the garden without a house. She told it at every opportunity and Keith had to admit that her very way of talking made the silly story sound interesting.

He had to be fair and admit also to himself that her interest in the garden was genuine. She had what he'd heard his mother refer to as green fingers. She could make anything grow.

His head told him that her interest was in the garden but his heart didn't. He kept seeing in his mind's eye that good-looking, fair-haired young man leaning on his hoe.

However, it was not until two weeks later that Sheila actually suggested they go back.

"I'd like to see how he's getting on. I have some plants . . ."

"No!"

At his tone, Sheila's head jerked up. She'd just made him a cup of coffee as he sat on a high stool at the end of the kitchen table in her home.

The rest of her family were watching television in the living-room.

"Keith . . ." She sounded as if she didn't believe him.

"I said no! I've put up with a lot, but I'm not trailing back to see a man I don't know and look at a garden I'm not even interested in."

Sheila laid down her own cup and her expression changed. All the liveliness died out of her face.

"What do you mean — you've put up with a lot?" she asked carefully.

"Well . . ." Infuriatingly, now he was faced with the direct question, he couldn't think of anything definite to say. It wasn't that Sheila had done all that much. It was just the way she was!

"You're far too friendly with strangers," he said lamely at last.

First Kiss

AS we kissed in the moonlit garden
  On that far-off velvet night,
Your lips were soft as petals
  In the moth-brushed mystic light.

Was it only the stars' reflection
  I saw in your dear eyes?
Ah no, 'twas the love-light shining,
  The kind that never dies.

As we tiptoed among the flowers,
  Long ago, on a night like this,
I lost my heart for ever
  In the spell of our first kiss.

Violet Hall.

"Am I indeed?" There was a gleam in her eyes. "I don't remember you complaining about my friendliness on the day we met. We were strangers then. But if you're not pleased with me the way I am, perhaps you'd better find someone else."

"I didn't mean that at all."

"There's no need to shout!"

"I'm not shouting!"

Things went from bad to worse and this time they parted frigidly.

KEITH spent the most miserable week of his life, certain only of one thing as time went on — that he wanted Sheila on any terms — because, no matter what, she was the only girl for him.

It took him that whole week to summon up enough courage to phone her. But when he finally did it was her mother who answered.

"I'm sorry, Keith, but she's not in. She's gone to visit some old lady in hospital."

"Do you know which hospital? I could go and meet her."

"I don't. She said something about a garden . . ."

"I see." Keith replaced the phone and turned away.

That garden! He swore at it long and fluently in his mind. The old woman could only be the aunt of that character Ramage. But how had she found out which hospital the old lady was in?

It was a stupid question. Sheila would find out about it just as she always found out about anything, by asking. She'd probably asked that very afternoon in the garden. The very idea of some old lady

72

permanently in hospital would be enough to make Sheila feel she should go and visit her.

Probably the truth was that the old woman had dozens of relations. No doubt Alan Ramage was visiting her, too. He certainly would be if he hoped to inherit the house, Keith thought sourly. No doubt he and Sheila would meet at the bedside!

O NE week crept into another, but on the Friday Keith could stand it no longer. His work was suffering. He couldn't concentrate. All he could think about was Sheila.

He phoned the house again and Sheila answered herself.

"Hello." Was he imagining it or was there still a hint of frostiness in her voice?

"Sheila — please — I must see you."

"Keith — I've been so miserable."

His heart gave a dizzy lurch, because there was no frost after all.

"I'll come round tonight."

"Not tonight. I'm sorry."

"Tomorrow, then. We'll have a picnic — go back to the same place beside the river."

"Darling . . ." She hesitated.

"Keith, I have to go to that garden — just for a couple of hours," she went on with a breathless rush. "You won't mind."

"A couple of hours!" He was incensed. "A couple of hours!" he said again, as if he couldn't believe the sound of his own voice.

"I just want to . . ."

"No," he said loudly, and stopped for two reasons. One was that he couldn't trust himself to say anything more and the other was that she had hung up on him.

Keith spent an even more miserable night than he had before, sitting sleepless in his bedroom in the flat he shared with two friends.

He had believed that Sheila had loved him and him only. This was like one of those awful nightmares where you get lost and can't find the way out.

He had truly believed that he'd changed, that he wanted Sheila on her terms — on any terms — but if she wanted to spend two hours in that garden, it must be because she wanted to see Alan Ramage.

Keith finally fell asleep before dawn and wakened feeling as if he had never been asleep at all, his mouth dry and his eyes gritty. He regarded himself without pleasure as he shaved. His face was white and his black hair untidy. There were bags beneath his eyes and his mouth drooped downwards.

He had lost all confidence in himself. He'd never in his life felt like this before.

His friends didn't interest him and he wanted to be by himself. That wasn't true, either. He wanted to be with Sheila.

As for Alan Ramage, a man with whom he himself had never exchanged two words — Keith broke off his thoughts and made his way purposefully to where he had parked his car.

H E reached the village and, half a mile beyond it, the garden. Today the sun was not shining and it was threatening rain. Keith parked the car at the gate and got out. He saw Sheila at once, weeding the herbaceous border, a blue scarf over her red hair. There was no sign of Alan Ramage.

"Sheila . . ."

She straightened and stood looking at him. He saw she seemed pale and unhappy. He had never loved her so much as he did at that moment.

"Darling . . ." he began.

She dropped the trowel and he gathered her into his arms.

"It was all my fault," he went on. "You can come to this garden every Saturday if you like."

For the moment, he really meant it. Sheila smiled, the dimple deepened at the corner of her mouth, and his heart gave its usual leap. She clung to him and the wind caught the scarf she had round her head, lifting it off and draping it over a rose bush several yards away.

"You're cold. I have coffee in the car. We could even —" he swallowed and made a great effort "— give Alan Ramage a cup." He looked round. "Where is he?"

"At home. He fell off his bicycle and broke his ankle. He has it in plaster, his aunt told me. She asked me to come today and tidy up and I said I would. I didn't really want to, but I promised and you didn't give me time to explain."

"She asked you!" Keith gaped at her. "She had a nerve!"

"She's been a great gardener all her days. It's what keeps her going in hospital, she says, thinking about the garden here. She meant to do up the cottage herself one day and live here, but she could never afford it. That's what she says anyway, but I really think it's just been like a dream to her."

Sheila paused, and when Keith said nothing, she went on.

"She's going to give Alan Ramage the house right away, because he wants to get married to some girl in Stirling."

It had started to rain but it seemed to Keith that the sun had come out.

"Sheila, how do you manage to find out so much about people you hardly know?"

It was a question which didn't really need an answer, because he already knew it. Sheila knew because she asked, and she asked because she loved people and was interested in them.

And he loved her. He loved every bit of her and he wouldn't want to change her by an inch.

Here he found he was smiling again and he put his arm around Sheila and hurried her to the shelter of the car, because the rain was now a downpour.

He was deluding himself. He knew he was. Sheila would exasperate him many a time, but, well — undoubtedly he would exasperate her, too.

It was all the fault of this thing, this unpredictable thing, called love. □

Too Many Memories

by
Clare Gibbon

"YOU'LL find it quiet at this time of year," the proprietor of the small hotel said as she led Jane upstairs.

"Yes. I expect I will," Jane replied.

After walking the length of a corridor, the woman threw open a door at the end and stood to one side allowing Jane to enter.

"I could have given you a larger room, but at the back with no sea view."

Jane felt the woman's eyes upon her as she crossed to the window.

"No thank you, this will be fine," she heard herself say in a rather clipped reserved tone.

"Bathroom's round the corner. The fire escape's . . ."

Jane shivered involuntarily.

"You're cold!" The woman exclaimed moving to the electric wall fire and switching it on. "As I was saying, the fire escape's through the door on the right and dinner's six thirty to seven thirty. You will be having dinner won't you?"

"Perhaps. I don't know." Jane was tired after the train journey and was becoming irritated by the woman's persisting presence.

"It's all good home cooking." A defensive note had crept into her voice. "I doubt if you'll find anywhere else open this early. It's only a small place you know, not like . . ."

"Yes, I know," interrupted Jane and turning her back on the woman, bit into her bottom lip in an effort to control herself.

"I'm sorry. I thought maybe you didn't realise. If you'll excuse me . . ." The door closed softly.

The single divan bed was covered with floral-printed cotton which matched the curtains at the window. It wasn't unlike Sarah's little room

75

back home, where she'd been sleeping since last summer's tragedy.

Resisting the urge to throw herself on the bed and drown in the oblivion of tears, she flung open her suitcase and took out a pair of jeans and two thick sweaters.

The sand was firm beneath the soles of her flat shoes. Swirls of mist drifted around her and the cold wind bit into her face and blew through her loose hair. Keeping her eyes down, she thrust her hands deep into the pockets of her woollen jacket.

She knew if only she were to breathe deeply and throw out her arms, she'd find it exhilarating and bracing. But she'd not come here to be exhilarated or braced, though she wasn't at all sure why she had come.

"I'd much rather you waited a while until we could go together," Tony had urged. "I'm not at all happy about you going back there alone. It's . . . well, it's morbid."

"Maybe it is, but I'm going anyway."

"How about . . . if I come up and join you Friday evening?"

"No, Tony!" she'd replied unreasonably. "I just want to be on my own. Besides, I shan't go anywhere near where we were. The hotel's at the other end." She'd turned from the pleading in Tony's eyes.

JUST then, as if conjured up from the mist, a large golden Labrador bounded towards her and skidding to a halt a few feet away, dropped a rubber ball from its mouth.

With tongue hanging out and appeal in its eyes, it looked from her to the ball at its feet.

Feeling affronted by this intrusion into her private world, she walked on, ignoring it. It whimpered softly as she passed by.

Some yards further on, where the mist was particularly thick, she thought she saw a dark shape passing between her and the sea. Amidst the plaintive cries of seagulls overhead and the constant crashing of the waves some distance off, she thought she heard someone say "Good evening," but couldn't be sure.

Her cheeks were smarting and her fingers tingling when she eventually clambered up the sandy embankment and scrambled back across the sand dunes towards the small hotel.

Along the coastline a few lights were visible through the mist, landmarks of the small fishing village. Perhaps she'd go as far as the harbour tomorrow.

Several tables in the dining-room were occupied. As she was shown to her solitary place by the window, she gathered the impression the other guests were all elderly and in parties of two or more. At least there were no children, of that she'd made certain.

THERE was little sound in the hotel as she let herself out early next morning.

Crossing the sand dunes, she paused by one or two sheltered spots, trying to recall where they'd picnicked last year. It wasn't possible to be sure as so many of them looked the same.

It was still too early in the year for there to be much litter about, but she scuffed her shoe on a half buried drinks can, and a torn crisp bag scuttled across her path, carried along by the wind.

The mist was less dense this morning and blew in soft swirls, clearing now and then to give glimpses of the huge expanse of cold grey sea.

The tide was right in, and there was only a narrow stretch of soft sand for her to walk along. It spilled over into her shoes and crouching to remove them, she saw the red handle of a child's spade.

Without realising what she was doing, she began frantically digging away the sand round the half buried spade until she had it in her grasp. Sarah's had been red too, just like this one. Jane remembered buying it at the little shop beside the cafe on the front.

The unrelenting pain tore at her again and she wondered if it would ever ease as people promised.

She was still on her knees remembering, when a scurry of movement and a shower of soft sand, heralded the arrival of a clumsy four-legged intruder in the shape of the golden Labrador she'd seen the previous evening.

JANE scrambled to her feet as the creature threatened to bowl her over in its excitement. The red spade fell from her grasp and before she could retrieve it, the Labrador, after a few short yelps of welcome, sniffed at the bright object, picked it up between its teeth, turned heel and disappeared into the mist.

"Here!" she shouted fruitlessly after the animal, before tears of frustration prevented her calling further.

"Morning there!" The greeting came from some distance away. She looked up to see the shape of a man approaching through the mist.

Without stopping to think she turned and hastily retraced her steps, moving as quickly as she could without actually running. She only stopped to replace her shoes once she was up on the sand dunes in sight of the hotel.

Later that morning, Jane took a packed lunch and went in the direction of the tiny harbour. The mist had cleared, the wind had dropped and it was a calm, but dull day.

The smell of salt air mingled with that of fish and disused lobster pots as she made her way along the curved jetty.

She knew that here she could soak herself in memory watching these men at work without them making any intrusion into her thoughts. It was here that Tony and she had brought Sarah each day . . . each day until that fateful evening at the end of the holiday . . . the end of everything.

Her eyes fell on the newly painted trawler "Pretty Princess." How Sarah would have loved the new bright colours which now adorned the smallest fishing vessel in the harbour.

"Named a'ter the likes o' you, she be," the corpulent fisherman had told his inquisitve observer last year, peering up at her with laughing eyes. "Pretty Princess!" he'd drawled the words, thumping her wooden frame with his fist before stooping and giving his attention once more to his precious cargo.

Sarah had been delighted and had skipped off along the narrow jetty to pester someone else. She or Tony had never been far from her side, always watchful that she didn't go too near the edge or too near the heavy lorries which trundled along the jetty collecting the boxes of freshly caught fish.

All her short life they'd been constantly vigilant. Except for that once. That one snatched half hour after Sarah had gone to bed, when the magic of the setting sun had lured them away, down to the water's edge, out of sight, out of hearing . . .

Jane closed her eyes in an attempt to blot out the terrible image blazing once more before her eyes.

SOMETHING warm and soft was sniffing round her ankles and standing quite still, she slowly opened her eyes. The golden Labrador, its curiosity satisfied, sat directly in her path. It gave a few short yelps of welcome much as it had done that morning, then sat watching for her response, its tail wagging furiously.

Approaching her, was a grey-haired man wearing dark glasses.

"Sandy!" the man said quietly.

The dog whimpered softly but stayed its ground.

Jane, though uncomfortably aware of being trapped, felt that she was experiencing something special here between master and dog. Rather reluctantly, she stepped to one side.

"Please stay awhile," the man said, stopping beside her. "You must be the new friend Sandy's come across on our walks." There was no question in his remark, rather an amused satisfaction in his discovery. "You're a visitor, aren't you?"

"Yes," Jane heard herself say.

"Don't get many this time of year. Least not down on the beach. Sandy here," he put his hand out and fondled one of the dog's silken ears, "gets to think he owns the whole place."

"Yes." Jane moved to one side to allow an elderly fisherman to pass. He tilted his cap and she winced as she saw the flicker of recognition across his face. It was a small place. Tragedies would not be easily forgotten.

Perhaps he would have stopped and spoken, but the man with the dog was talking to her.

"We're just on our way home," he was saying. "Care to walk with us awhile?"

Jane looked away from the man's weather-beaten face. He had such an easy, friendly way about him, that she found herself feeling ashamed at the way she'd run away from him that morning.

"Or maybe you've something else planned?" he was saying.

"No, no," she managed. "Yes. I'll walk a little way."

Companionably, they made their way off the jetty and began walking along the front beside the sea wall, Sandy between them.

" 'Morning, Jack!" Several locals called out and raised their caps to her. Always he replied with a raised arm and cheery greeting.

"My wife's back at the cottage. Would you come and take a cup of tea with us?'' Jack asked, as if it were the most natural thing in the world.

But Jane had been growing apprehensive ever since they'd left the jetty. It seemed Jack's home was in the opposite direction to the hotel and if she were to go much further . . .

"No! No thank you," she said hastily. "I really must get back," she lied. "I've . . . I've a phone call to make."

"Ah, well!'' He didn't persist and for that she was grateful. Standing quite still, he put out his hand. "Now that we've become acquainted, we'll be looking out for you, won't we, Sandy?'' again there was a gentle air of amusement in his voice.

Jane put her hand in his and felt the firm handshake. Any disquiet or irritation she'd felt towards the man and his dog had been completely dispelled and she felt a strange sense of peace. There was something about them . . . something special which she couldn't quite put her finger on.

Jane was disappointed that evening as she walked the deserted beach and saw no sign of Jack or his dog. She even found herself searching for their footprints in the firm sand, but there were only the spidery thin prints of numerous birds.

Someone Special

FLOWERS on a sweet bouquet,
I send you on this special day.
May the message of each flower,
Bring my love for every hour.
Throughout all my childhood days,
You have cherished me always;
Shared my laughter, dried my tears,
Steadfast through the changing years.
Guided me in paths anew
Taught me all that's good and true.
How can any words express
All this love and happiness?
Thank you, Mother dear, I pray,
God bless you, this and every day.

Dorothy M. Loughran.

She thought perhaps he'd be walking along the other end of the beach near his home, though he'd stressed how Labradors required a great deal of exercise.

Eventually she gave up looking and turned towards the warm, welcoming hotel lights.

NEXT morning Jane awoke to the sound of rain lashing against her window and she turned over, pulling the bedclothes over her head.

It was late afternoon before the rain ceased and, thankful that she'd brought her wellington boots, she set off along the wet sands.

A high tide had brought up unusually large amounts of seaweed and picking up a strand of the greeny-brown material, she remembered Sarah's enthusiasm for it last year.

Tony had hung some on a low nail outside the cottage and each morning Sarah had tested it for dampness, then predicted the forecast accordingly. But even that treasured piece of seaweed had been irretrievable after the terrible holocaust.

79

Jane's heart ached with the memory of it all so that she barely noticed the incoming tide was sloshing around her feet. She stood with her back to the sea, hand shielding her eyes and scanned the beach in both directions. There was no sign of anyone. Nothing but sea and sand and more sea and more sand.

She didn't stop by the harbour where a few locals were busy about their boats, but hurried on, scrambling back down onto the beach at the first available pathway. It was only if she stayed up on top that round the next bend the burned out shell would be visible. From down on the beach it would be hidden by the sandy embankment.

IN the distance Jane caught sight of a figure walking towards her, dog at heel. It was only as they drew nearer that she realised with disappointment that the dog was a terrier and the figure that of a woman. She remembered them now from last year. They'd passed once or twice, right in front of the cottage.

Afraid of being recognised, Jane waded into the shallow water and remained there with her back to the woman until she'd disappeared in the direction of the harbour.

Before finally turning in the direction of the hotel, she had one last look along the beach, then allowed her gaze to travel along the top of the embankment where it met the darkening sky. A sudden movement stopped her in her tracks.

A splash of gold, darker than the sand was slithering down the steep slope. She kept her eyes on the skyline, waiting for Jack to follow in the dog's wake, but he didn't appear and she was still waiting when Sandy came bounding up to her.

He romped around her in circles barking excitedly, then running a little way off as if inviting her to follow. Eventually, after much tail wagging and dog language which she didn't understand, he scampered off. She watched him run up the embankment, over the top and out of sight.

That night Jane tossed and turned and when she did finally fall into a fitful sleep, she relived the terrible nightmare of last year, only this time Jack and Sandy were there, stretching out, as if trying to reach her.

It was late next morning when she finally rose but her mind was clear and she knew what she must do.

It was only as she passed the harbour that she realised how little she had to go on. She didn't know where Jack and his wife lived. But most people had seemed to know him and there were few enough dwellings along this stretch.

She was already alongside the short golf course where a few figures were dotted about, but it was towards the clump of tall trees at the far end that she was looking.

She knew their screen couldn't last much longer. Any moment now the charred shell would become visible, its skeleton roof framed against the sky in stark reminder of what had been.

She wanted to look anywhere but there, yet a magnetism stronger than herself, held her gaze fixed on one spot.

C OMING into sight now was a rooftop, but not one of bare, burnt rafters as she remembered. This was a newly tiled roof, not yet quite completed. It was only as the whole building came into view that she saw the caravan parked at the far side.

There was movement in the overgrown garden. As she watched, a stooped figure straightened up and walked towards the cottage, entering it through a gaping hole that had once been a front door under a shower of trailing roses.

Someone was rebuilding the cottage. She stood quite still, stunned by the realisation of her discovery.

The figure, which was that of a woman in late middle age re-emerged as Jane found herself walking slowly forward.

There was an old wooden shed at the bottom of the garden and leaning against it she tried to take in the scene before her. To think that anyone should take on the challenge of re-building such a wreck.

It was then that the woman caught sight of her.

"Hello there!" she called.

"Hello." Jane called back feebly.

"Care for a cuppa? I'm parched and ready for a breather myself," the woman called as she came towards her.

"Thank you. That would be nice." Jane, still dazed remained where she was, leaning against the shed.

"My name's Dolly. Dolly Wilson. We're living in the caravan just now," she jerked her thumb toward it, "until we've finished rebuilding. Come and look."

Jane found herself following Dolly Wilson, as she led her through the overgrown garden into what remained of the cottage.

"It's not very big," she was saying. "Only two rooms other than the kitchen and bathroom. You can even see what the wallpaper was like in here." She peeled off a strip of the rose-patterned paper which Jane remembered so well.

The main dividing wall, which held a fireplace at each side and which had partly collapsed at the time, had not yet been repaired. Jane shivered.

"Come on. Let's have that cuppa. You'll have to excuse my husband," she called over her shoulder as she went towards the caravan. "He's got a touch of flu and isn't dressed yet." She paused on the steps to the caravan before opening the door.

"Sandy!" she called, her voice carrying far. "Wretched dog! Has to exercise himself with Jack not being well."

Jane felt a smile spread over her face. It had been so long since she'd had anything to smile about that she'd almost forgotten how to smile.

Sandy appeared and, after a hasty sniff round her ankles, yelped his now familiar welcome.

"I've brought a young woman to cheer you up," Dolly Wilson was saying, as Jack, still wearing dark glasses was moving down the caravan with an ease of knowledge of his surroundings.

With a warm smile on his lips, he extended a hand and Jane took it eagerly.

F

"Good morning," he said. "So, Sandy tracked you down, then."

Before long, the trio were sitting comfortably drinking tea and eating home-baked scones, while Sandy, stretched out on the floor waited eagerly for any crumbs coming his way.

"When Jack had to take early retirement with the loss of his sight, we both felt we needed a challenge." Dolly Wilson put her hand over her husband's on the table.

"And we've always wanted to live on the sea front, haven't we, love?" Jack asked.

"We have." She smiled, letting Jack take up the story.

"Mind you, though I've been in the building trade all my life, I am finding that roof a mite tricky," he chuckled softly.

"There's nothing in this life that's all plain sailing," Dolly remarked pouring out more tea.

Listening to them, Jane felt calmer and more at peace than she had done for a long, long time. But she also felt ashamed.

"You're right," she whispered. "There's nothing all plain sailing."

She watched as Dolly squeezed Jack's hand, but the woman remained silent.

Though they'd asked her nothing, in some strange, uncanny way, Jane felt they understood.

"I hope you'll come again," Jack was saying as she prepared to leave.

"Yes, do." His wife got up from the table. "We'd love to see you at any time."

"Thank you." Jane replied. "Maybe I will." She'd go back to the hotel now and ask the proprietor if that larger room was still available, she decided.

"I've to phone my husband," she continued. "He may be joining me tomorrow."

Making her way back through the neglected garden, she paused at the sight of a single white rose struggling to survive among the waist-high weeds. Touched by its loveliness, she stooped to sample its frangrance, then turned, and smiling again, waved farewell to Jack and Dolly Wilson and their dog, Sandy.

One day, perhaps before too long, this garden would be restored to a beauty it had once known, not so very long ago. □

Lochinch Castle, near Stranraer in Wigtownshire, is a relatively young castle. It was built in Scottish baronial style for the Earls of Stair and was completed in 1876. It replaced their former home, Castle Kennedy, which was destroyed by fire in 1716. The magnificent gardens of Lochinch are open to the public and are famous for their rare shrubs. Rhododendrons and azaleas are a speciality of these beautiful grounds, which were laid out by the second Earl of Stair, whose inspiration was Versailles.

LOCHINCH CASTLE : J CAMPBELL KERR

MARGARET CLARKSON lifted the tickets from the mantelpiece and looked at them, shaking her head. One pound, fifty pence each for afternoon tea — it was ridiculous! Of course, there was to be a fashion show and a celebrity guest, whoever that might be, but it was still a lot of money.

The trouble is, she admitted to herself, when you're going to be seventy the following Saturday as she was, you can't just forget about the price of things. Still, the Women's Rural Institute knew how to organise things and they'd make it a lovely afternoon.

Both she and Betty Anderson were looking forward to the outing. The two women had become close friends since Margaret's son, Gerald, had married Betty's daughter.

SOMETHING TO CELEBRATE

by Kathleen Kinmond

In fact, the afternoon tea had been Betty's idea — she'd suggested it as a treat for Margaret's coming birthday. They were lucky, too, in that they didn't have to worry about transport to the little village hall. Alec, Margaret's husband, was only too willing to drive them. He knew he could visit a farmer friend while they were at the afternoon tea.

But Margaret was still a little worried about the expense. She'd discussed it with Alec only that lunch-time.

"Don't worry so much," he'd said easily, "just be grateful to Betty for wanting to give you this treat. She did offer to pay, didn't she?"

"Yes, that's just the trouble." Margaret sighed. "She can't afford to throw money away like that, now she's on her own." Betty's husband had died only a year before.

"Well, it's her birthday present to you, so you'll just have to accept it graciously," Alec told her.

"I must admit I am looking forward to Saturday." Margaret smiled. "It's very good of our Gerald and his wife to give me the party at their house, although I'm sorry the rest of the children can't come too."

Even though their family was now grown up and had their own homes, she still liked to call them the children, when she and Alec were alone.

"Mmm," Alec said between mouthfuls of pudding, "but you can't have everything, and they all have their own lives to lead, you must remember. Apparently neither Danny nor Katie could break the arrangements they'd already made."

"Oh, I know," she said. Her children always kept their word — she and Alec had brought them up that way. But she knew they'd be disappointed that they couldn't be with her.

GERALD, their first born, was the only one who lived in the same city as they did. Then there was Danny, who lived in Morayshire, and Katie, their youngest, whose home was in Edinburgh with her husband and two little daughters.

Grant, the second eldest boy, was the only unmarried one. He'd been in the West Indies now for almost twenty years but he came home at regular intervals to see them all and for any special family occasion.

He's forty-two now, Margaret mused, and although he's a successful businessman, he's just as kind and considerate now as he was when he was young. He made sure his parents didn't go short of anything in their retiral.

The year his father retired he'd come home for a short visit.

"I'll be mailing you a monthly cheque, starting next month," he'd said casually, the morning he was due to fly back.

When his father had protested and said they'd be all right, there was no argument, but the cheques came regularly just the same. He didn't have a wife and children to spend his money on, was the only argument he put up.

"Grant's cheques have certainly come in useful," Alec said, and

Margaret marvelled again at the way his words always echoed her own thoughts. "We'd never have been able to have that holiday in Sorrento last month without them."

"You're right," she agreed. "It's amazing the extra luxuries it's brought us."

She sat down beside her husband, taking up very little room. She was a tiny, unbelievably young almost-seventy-year-old. Alec was fond of telling anyone who'd listen that it was her tininess and neatness which had made him fall in love with her all those years ago. She'd been a good, loving wife, bringing up the three boys single handed when he'd been away during the Second World War. And, although times must have been tight on a soldier's pay, she'd never complained.

"Sometimes I wish Grant would find himself a lovely wife like the other boys have," she said thoughtfully. "We're so lucky to have two such super daughters-in-law. I'd like to see him settled too."

"Get away with you," her husband said teasingly, "you're just an old mother hen, still fussing over your brood. Grant seems perfectly happy and fulfilled to me. Maybe he just hasn't met the right girl yet."

O N the Saturday of the fashion show, Margaret dressed carefully in her best silky dress, for, as Betty had explained, it could well be quite a smart affair.

Alec and Margaret picked up Betty in their car and all three enjoyed the run out to the little country hall where the Rural held its meetings.

"Now, I'm simply not going to let you pay all this," Margaret was protesting to her friend as they arrived at the hall. "It's far too much."

"Oh, I don't know," Betty said mildly. "I believe it's to be well worth it. Anyway, if you're still in the same mind, we can talk about it later."

There were a few cars already parked outside, but otherwise it seemed surprisingly quiet.

It was only when Alec pushed the door open for Margaret and Betty to enter that she heard the sound of movement and then suddenly she could see rows of familiar faces. They all burst into song when they saw Margaret.

"Happy birthday to you, happy birthday to you, happy birthday, dear Mother," some sang, and others, "dear Margaret."

She stood still, both hands on her face as she took in the happy scene of her entire family. Gerald and Danny, both with their wives and children, Katie with her husband and little girls, and yes — there was Grant, too, dear Grant who'd flown all that distance, just to be with them all on this happy day.

"Well, dear," said Alec's proud voice in her ear, "what do you think of this surprise?"

"Wonderful, just wonderful," she said when she could trust herself to speak, "and as well as our own family, I can see aunties and uncles and friends — old friends that we've had all our lives," and only then did her voice break a little.

After she'd been soundly hugged and kissed by everyone, she

noticed the banner emblazoned from one side of the hall to the other.

"Happy Birthday, Mum," it proclaimed in enormous letters, and under that in slightly smaller print, "1910-1980. We *love* you."

Hastily she blinked back a tear and turned to Betty, who was at her side.

"And what about this fashion show and the celebrity guest we were to meet here this afternoon, you scamp?" she scolded her friend, a catch in her voice.

"That was yourself, of course." Betty laughed. "And don't blame me, anyway. It was your first born who had the tickets printed."

"Really, Gerald?" Margaret asked her son, who was nearby. "Did you honestly go to all that trouble? But they were real, honest-to-goodness tickets." She couldn't hide her surprise.

"Yes, a pal of mine did half a dozen." He grinned. "I thought he made a jolly good job of them."

A ND you never suspected a thing?" Alec asked, as they wandered round together, arm in arm, meeting the guests.

"I must admit I had to bite my tongue time and time again when I almost gave away the secret." He confessed. "And all the telephoning that had to be done between Morayshire, Edinburgh and here — I was sure you'd guess."

"I hadn't even an inkling." She giggled. "I don't know how you did it — you seem to have invited all my favourite people, too . . . I'd liked to have seen Granny Smail, though, but I can't expect you to have remembered everyone."

"But we invited her," Alec said. "Isn't she here?"

"Not that I can see." Margaret looked around.

"I wonder what can have happened?" he said, almost to himself. As Margaret's two sisters-in-law came up to claim her attention, he excused himself and wandered thoughtfully to the door. Opening the heavy wooden door, he looked hopefully outside to the row of parked cars.

"Anything wrong, Dad?" a voice asked. He turned to see his son, Grant.

"I don't know," Alec replied. "We asked Granny Smail but she hasn't turned up."

"Look, give me her address and I'll dash into town and see if she's all right," Grant suggested. "I'm really dying to try out that car I hired yesterday. I haven't really had much of a chance to test it."

"That would be fine if you could, son." His father cheered up. "I know your mother will be disappointed if the old lady can't make it."

G RANT settled himself behind the wheel of the fast white car and soon it was humming quietly on its way to the city.

Granny Smail. He smiled as he remembered the neighbour to whom they'd all run when they'd had an "accident" and needed a quick stitch in the seat of their pants before their mother discovered it, or their faces given a quick wipe when they'd failed to keep clean, as ordered.

The road was quiet and empty but even so he didn't notice the Mini until it was right on him. Both cars had to brake quickly to avoid an accident.

He jumped out of the car immediately, knowing he had been too far over on the wrong side of the road.

THE driver of the Mini was a very pretty, dark-haired girl, probably in her early thirties, very petite and dainty, and suddenly Grant found himself lost for words. They stared at each other for a few seconds, without speaking, until a voice broke the silence.

"It's Grant Clarkson, isn't it? I might have known! You were always in a hurry."

"Granny Smail!" Grant cried delightedly, leaning into the car and giving her a hug. "I was actually on my way to see what had held you up!"

"Oh, it was my son's car," the old woman explained. "It never starts when it has to. Goodness knows what's wrong with it this time. He phoned Jennifer's folk across the road from me and she came over to tell me and, bless her, offered to run me out."

"Great. So all's well that ends well!" he exclaimed, and turned to Jennifer.

"Grant Clarkson," he introduced himself.

"Jennifer Leslie," she replied, and as she smiled he thought how attractive she was. The pale-blue open-necked blouse and trousers to match gave her a fresh appearance.

"Well, I suppose I can hand over my passenger to you here," she said, in a warm, friendly voice.

"No, no," Mrs Smail said hastily. "I don't think I'd like to trust myself in that fast white thing. We were just doing fine, Jenny lass, if you don't mind."

Jennifer grinned to Grant and winked mischievously.

"What do you say to that, Mr Clarkson?" she asked.

"Grant, please," he replied, "and I'd say it's a great idea. Perhaps you'd like to come to the party, too."

"Oh, I couldn't possibly do that," she said quickly. "I'm not dressed for a party, and besides I haven't been invited."

"You look just perfect to me," Grant said admiringly, "and knowing my mother, she wouldn't like you to go off home without her being able to thank you for bringing Mrs Smail."

The latter, sitting demurely in the passenger seat, smiled knowingly. It seemed Grant wasn't quite so shy with women as his mother had suggested.

When they arrived at the hall, all the Clarkson family came up to greet the old lady and Grant seized the opportunity to introduce Jennifer to his mother."

"Of course you must stay," Margaret said at once. "It was so good of you giving up your afternoon to bring Granny Smail here."

BY now, everyone was seated at the meal, and what a meal. Danny, a chef, had planned the meal and he and the family had worked with a will to prepare a really sumptuous buffet.

Turkey, ham and roast beef all graced the laden table, flanked by at least a dozen different kinds of salad.

Jewel-like sweets waited patiently at the end of the long table for the second course, looking rather overawed by a handsome stilton to finish the meal.

Old friends who hadn't met for many years exchanged conversation across the table, and all round the table was the happy sound of carefree chatter and shared jokes.

Occasionally, in the background, could be heard Betty's young doctor son trying out the rather elderly piano, with another guest and Gerald on the accordion and violin, so that by the time the floor was cleared of the tables, they were able to draw the company on to the floor, with tune after tune of the Roarin' Twenties and the decade before the war.

THE ROSE

'TIS a rose that sunwards rears its
head
Within the garden sanctuary.
Knows dawns and sunsets, gentle rain and mellow sunshine. Till comes the fullness of its glory.
Alas! As by the shears of Fate, the stem is snipped.
The rose is riven from its happy home.
For what?
To enter on a second glory.
A thing of beauty, to cheer the widow's lonely home.
Bright flag of courage by some patient's bed, to rally in the desperate struggle for recovery.
Is life a rose to bloom for its own pleasure in a private Eden?
Life too has its second glory, when given to cheer and strengthen those in need.

Rev. T. R. S. Campbell.

Delighted guests found themselves singing and dancing to old, familiar songs.

It was Katie, they discovered, who had scoured Edinburgh until she'd found an old song book with the numbers which their mother had sung to them, as children. And she thoroughly enjoyed leading everyone in each song.

"Who is the pretty young woman who brought you here?" Margaret wanted to know of Agnes Smail, as she watched the girl dancing round with most of the male members of the company, particularly Grant.

"Jennifer Leslie," she explained, with a broad smile. "You know her mother, Janet Wilkie. Remember, Jennifer was a late baby and the cleverest of the lot. She's a lawyer, you know, and what a nice girl."

"Is she married?" Margaret couldn't stop herself from asking.

"No," Granny Smail's smile wavered. "She was engaged to another lawyer in the same office but it was broken off just at Christmas time, poor lass."

Margaret opened her mouth to comment but just then Danny's son,

Philip, announced he was going to play some recordings which he thought would interest his grandmother, and of course his grandfather, too.

The recording started and Margaret gasped with delight at the voice of her sister, Jean, sending birthday greetings from Australia. But this was only the beginning, for more recordings followed from different parts of Britain. Philip had contacted many of their old friends and it became a lively competition to see who could recognise the voices first.

"Well, wasn't that a surprise?" Alec said afterwards to Margaret. "That kid must have started months ago to have it ready for today. Even I didn't know that all that preparation was going on."

JENNIFER LESLIE watched the happy faces around her and thought what a lucky chance it was that she'd offered to drive Mrs Smail here — she hadn't enjoyed herself as much for ages. Nobody, young or old, was allowed to sit out any dances. Aunties, uncles and friends, all were persuaded on to the dance floor by enthusiastic youngsters.

"What a super family the Clarksons are," she said enthusiastically to Bob Bruce, a friend of Alec's, during a Paul Jones dance.

"They certainly are," he agreed.

"Alec and Margaret are very special people, and very good parents. Their children are a credit to them, too. We've known the boys since they were little.

"The Clarksons were never over-endowed with much money, but how happy they were and always so willing to share what little they had.

"But perhaps you know this already," he said, frightened he might be boring the girl.

"No, I don't," Jennifer replied. "I'm a stranger to the family," and quickly she explained the reason for her presence at the party.

"Please go on," she urged. "Tell me more about them."

"Well," he continued. "My wife and I were married a long time before our daughter was born. And one Christmas when we were a little down the Clarksons invited us to spend the time with them. They never mentioned it then but they knew how much we loved children and how disappointed we were that there was, as yet, no sign of a family.

"They told us," he continued, "years later, that they knew how much it would mean to us to spend Christmas in the company of children."

"Anyway, we had a marvellous time. On Christmas Eve, all seven of us went to a pantomime and we've never forgotten the boys eager little faces, fascinated by all that was happening on the stage and thoroughly enjoying every moment."

"And next morning?" Jennifer prompted.

"Oh, it was a wonderful sight, to see them delving into their stockings and the excited looks on their faces. Margaret and Alec had even filled stockings for us — we really felt like part of the family, that day."

He stopped and smiled at Jennifer, before continuing his story.

"Not long after that our own daughter was born, but we've never forgotten the Clarksons for their kindness to us."

Just then the music changed and they had to part. Grant made sure that he was her partner and Margaret, sitting this one out with Betty, noticed.

"Grant and that nice girl look good together, don't they?" she asked her friend.

"Yes," Betty agreed with a nod. "They do."

Talking to Alec during the next dance, Margaret repeated what she'd said to Betty.

"I just wish Grant could stay longer than the ten days he says he's allowed himself," she added. "But apparently there's a big business deal in the offing which he just can't miss. If there was only more time, I'm sure he and Jennifer Leslie . . ."

"Oh, Margaret dear." Alec laughed. "You're much too romantic. They've only known each other a few hours. How do you expect Grant, who's shown so little interest in girls, to fall in love so suddenly? Not only that, how do you know she's such a nice girl?"

"If Granny Smail says she's a nice girl," Margaret said evenly, "then she's a nice girl."

"Well, have it your own way, my love." Alec sighed. "But I think you're reading too much into it."

BY now the evening was drawing to a close, and as some of the guests had long distances to travel home, the women of the family were beginning to bring out cups and saucers for a last cup of tea and a slice of the beautifully-iced cake, baked by a family friend.

"Well, and how have you enjoyed your seventieth birthday party, Mother?" Grant asked, sitting down beside Margaret.

"Wonderful, just wonderful," she said simply. "Everything has been so carefully thought out and there's never been a dull moment."

She was silent for a moment and her eyes looked suspiciously bright. "To think you all went to such trouble and expense for my birthday . . . I don't know what to say."

Her voice broke and Grant put his hand gently over hers.

"What else did you expect, Mum?" he said, gently. "You've always been a super mother."

"I wish you could stay a little longer this time," she said wistfully. "You seem to be no sooner here than you're off."

He gave a little shrug.

"There always seems to be so much needing attending to," he said, then cleared his throat, a little nervously.

"Actually, I'm thinking of staying on another month." He said the words quickly.

"Another *month*!" She looked at him in delighted amazement. "But what about the big contract you're after?"

"Well, I've decided to let my assistant take care of that." He grinned. "I'd rather risk the contract than lose touch with a certain person."

His eyes went towards Jennifer Leslie who was sitting talking to some of the younger members of the family.

"Oh, Grant, I'm so glad," Margaret said delightedly. "I think you look so perfect together, even though you've just met. Tommy Smail's car was meant to break down. Your father says I'm just blethering, but I don't know." The words rushed out.

"I don't know either, Mother," he said, smiling down at her, "but I do know I've never met anyone before that I've liked so much."

Finally it was time to sing "Auld Lang Syne." But it wasn't to the accompaniment of the band, but to a recording by Margaret's sister and her husband, in Australia. Heartily, they all joined in.

Afterwards, by Alec's side, Margaret smiled warmly round the room at her friends and family, hoping they would realise she wasn't one for making speeches. She wished she was brave enough to do that — to thank her family for giving her such a wonderful time and her friends for sharing it with her, but that wasn't her way.

Later, perhaps with Alec's help, she'd find the words to thank all her family together, but for now she could only smile at each one in turn and hope her happiness shone through.

When her eyes alighted on Grant and Jennifer, she noted the way they looked at each other and her joy was complete. She squeezed Alec's hand and he followed the direction of her gaze.

"You were right, my love," he said, with a laugh. "As always."

It was a day neither would ever forget. And later when they climbed into the car for the journey home, and Alec turned to speak to her, she knew he would be able to voice the feelings she herself couldn't express.

"Some people have a lot of money," he said softly, "but our wealth lies in our family." There was a catch in his voice. "We're very lucky indeed."

Margaret could only nod in agreement. As always, he had put into words the very thoughts in her heart. □

93

TRY A LITTLE MAGIC

T HOUGH the daylight hours of early autumn retained some of their
warmth, the evenings were cool, forcing Joan MacLean and her
sister, Alison, to seek the warmth of the fireside. How welcome a
sight it was, too, with those multi-coloured flames licking round
crackling logs.

Joan had come from the town of Invermuir to Strathard to spend a few
days with her sister Alison, and her husband Bill, who was head teacher
of the local school. She stretched out her fingers to the warming flames
and sighed.

"I often wish I was back here, Alison, in Strathard. You and Bill seem
so content with life here."

by
Ian
Wilson

"I seem to remember you were always the restless one wanting to get away." Her elder sister laughed.

"Yes," Joan replied. "But there's always that little tug of the heart strings which says 'Go back.' "

She closed her eyes and her mind wandered back to those carefree days of childhood, cosseted and cared for by a loving mum and dad with the hills and glens their playground. What more could anyone want, Joan wondered. It seemed such a contrast to her busy job as the head of a small but thriving landscape gardening firm.

"I can still see the expression on Dad's face when you told him you wanted to be a landscape gardener like him," Alison replied, as if reading her thoughts.

Joan could even remember his words.

"But that's not lassie's work, Joan. You should be thinking of settling down to marry and have bairns." Joan had felt quite needled.

"Haven't you ever heard of Women's Lib, Dad?" she'd answered.

Alison smiled.

"I think he only let you do it because you thought you'd never make the grade," she added. "But there wasn't a prouder man than he the day you qualified."

THEY lapsed into silence, each occupied with their own private thoughts on the past. Alison, who'd wanted nothing in life but a home and family, and attractive, dark-haired Joan, seemingly ambitious, yet underneath it all, so vulnerable and able to be hurt deeply.

It was during the course of her work she had met Iain Hall, a young architect. There was something about him that seemed to mesmerise her. After their first date, there was another, and yet another.

Joan knew she was falling in love and she had no reason to doubt Iain's feelings. Soon they became inseparable and there was talk of an engagement. Joan felt on top of the world. She was about to have everything she'd always wanted — a career of her own and a loving marriage to give her security.

Though an engagement ring had been mentioned, Iain had evaded any discussion on the matter and Joan put this down to his being preoccupied with his work.

But the real truth came one evening when they were walking home under a sparkling canopy of stars, their arms round each other's waists.

"I'd like a ring darling, just to put the seal on our love," Joan had said impulsively.

Iain's hands had grown suddenly cold and he'd drawn away from her.

"Sorry, Joan, I should have told you before now, I suppose, but I'm not really the pipe-and-carpet-slippers type."

She'd stared at him in disbelief, her world crashing round about her.

"I suppose I shouldn't have started something I'd no intention of continuing," he'd continued embarrassedly. "I do feel rotten about it." Then almost as an afterthought he'd added, "I really would make a terrible husband."

At first, Joan had refused to believe him, but as time passed, she'd realised it was true that Iain's feelings had no depth. This knowledge, however, didn't ease her hurt, and though she'd flung herself into her work she was unable to forget that horrible moment. Now she'd come to Strathard for a few days partly to escape the charged atmosphere of Invermuir.

The hurt was still deep enough to bring tears to her eyes, something which didn't go unnoticed by Alison.

"If the weather's fine tomorrow why don't you take a walk up to the Trysting Pool?" she suggested.

"You were always one for the magic of that place, Alison." Joan smiled. "I doubt whether I'm receptive to magic spells at the moment."

NEXT morning, however, taking Alison's advice, Joan set off for a day in the hills. Alison had loaned her a pair of stout walking boots and in her haversack was a Thermos of coffee and some sandwiches.

A mile west of the town, she crossed the old humpbacked bridge, then turned on to the hill path. Some way beyond, Joan noticed the farmhouse partly hidden by a fold in the hills. Tofthill Farm, she remembered, I wonder who lives there now.

She pressed on determinedly till at last she stood once more by the Trysting Pool. It was a delightful haven of peace. The pool was deep and mysterious, set among silver birch and fern, and its most attractive feature was the waterfall which cascaded down the rocks behind and plunged with a roar into the pool. Nearby, the old wooden seat still remained, moss grown at the joints and rather decrepit. Joan sat down and looked around joyfully.

As the sounds about her took over, the hum of bees in the heather, wood pigeons cooing in the trees, Joan found her own turbulent thoughts fading away. For the first time in months she felt at peace.

Her mind drifted back to those dreamy days of childhood when she'd first come up here, and been fascinated by the shapes of the rocks and the mystery of the different plants. Those were the things that had made her dream of being like Dad, building, planting and shaping gardens. In her own mind, she designed what she called her own "Magic Places." She'd even thought that one day she'd design a special one for herself.

Thoughts of Iain suddenly rushed back. Now she knew that magic place she'd seemed so near to had all been a silly dream.

It was so easy to cry, and Joan did just that. But the tears weren't for Iain. Instead they were for her own foolishness in believing that life could be like a fairy tale.

She didn't hear footsteps, but then the soft springy turf on the track leading to the pool was like a deep pile carpet. A young man sat down on the seat beside her.

"I hope I'm not disturbing you," he said hesitantly.

Joan summoned up a smile in return. There was something about the young man's ready smile and sincerity in it which appealed to her.

"No, you didn't disturb me. This bench is meant for two. That's why

this place is called the 'Lovers' Tryst,' " she replied, informatively.
"I know, I've been here quite often."
As he spoke, Joan could sense an unhappiness about him.
"Are you here on holiday?" he asked.
"Yes, staying with my sister and her husband. Maybe you know
them. Strathard's not all that large. Alison and Bill Stevenson — my
brother-in-law is head teacher in the school."
He laughed but there was a brittle quality about it.
"Sorry, I don't have any connection with the school." His eyes
clouded as if what she'd said roused some painful memory. He stood up.
"Wish I could stay longer but it's a long way down the hill. Goodbye."
"Goodbye," Joan replied, but the memory of her encounter with the
stranger lingered until she returned to the house. She mentioned it to
Alison.
"I know the family," Alison told her. "Tim Paton runs the farm at
Tofthill. That's his son you met — Andrew. He works in the bank here
in Strathard. Such a tragedy though. His wife Nancy, such a lovely girl,
was killed in a riding accident a few months ago. They'd just moved into
a new house too. The poor man was completely broken up."
"I thought there was a sadness about him," Joan replied.

D URING the next few hectic days, Andrew Paton was forgotten
as Alison and Joan took advantage of the fine weather
to re-explore countryside Joan had almost forgotten.
As sisters, they'd always been close, and Alison was determined
that Joan should have no time to mope about Iain.
Her solution worked too. Joan returned to Invermuir feeling
refreshed and much more like her old self. In fact, she was looking
forward to getting back to work once more,doing a job which she really
adored. She realised with relief that she'd come through her recent crisis
only slightly bruised and a lot wiser. She thought of Andrew Paton and
his tragedy and realised just how lucky she was.
Planning and designing took up much of Joan's time. In between this
exacting work she took the opportunity to drive round and visit the jobs
her small team of men were working on. But now,though her work was
creative,Joan found that for some reason, each day left her with the
feeling of being unfulfilled. She felt lonely in the evenings in her empty
flat. The memories of happy times with Iain began to crowd in on her.
As they'd sat by the fireside, there had been something to look forward
to. Now there seemed to be nothing. What does the future hold for me,
she asked herself desperately.
Joan had just arrived home one evening when the phone rang. It was a
man's voice.
"Perhaps you don't remember me, Miss MacLean, but a few weeks
back we met briefly at the Trysting Pool. I'm Andrew Paton."
"Why yes, Mr Paton, I remember. What can I do for you?"
"I was talking to your brother-in-law in the bank the other day, Miss
MacLean. He told me about your line of business and I was wondering if
you would do some work for me. To be brief, I have a new house with a

garden that's completely derelict. In fact the garden hasn't been touched since I moved in. I was wondering if you'd like to have a look at it sometime with a view to constructing it for me."

"I'd be very pleased to, Mr Paton."

He supplied Joan with his address and they arranged to meet there on the Saturday afternoon. As she replaced the receiver, she suddenly felt her heart miss a beat.

Andrew was waiting anxiously for her arrival. He shook her hand warmly.

"I see you've come dressed for the occasion." He smiled.

"Standard equipment in my job," she replied. "Good, strong, warm slacks and wellington boots, with a warm anorak for good measure."

"It is rather chilly. Come inside and have some tea before you look at the garden." He ushered her inside. "Just a moment and I'll put the kettle on."

"Can I help?" Joan asked.

"Thanks, but I'll manage. I've had to become used to doing things for myself."

Again there was that cloud of sadness in his eyes. "Please make yourself at home, Miss MacLean, I shan't be a minute."

WHILE he made the tea, Joan glanced at her surroundings. The house was spacious and modern. The lounge was slightly untidy, but it was the painting above the mantelpiece that caught her attention.

"That's one of Nancy's paintings," Andrew told her, coming in with the tea tray.

"It's beautiful," Joan said. "She must have been very talented."

"Yes, she was. Painting, gardening, horse-riding . . ."

Joan noticed the sudden tremble of his fingers. "You heard about the accident I suppose?" he said.

"Yes, I'm very sorry."

Over tea they laughed about their first meeting. The conversation came round to Joan's childhood and her love of the countryside round Strathard.

"I always loved the Trysting Pool," she told Andrew. "I used to go there if I wanted something good to happen. I thought there was some kind of magic there, but I've grown up a lot since then."

"If you don't believe in magic any more, why were you at the pool that day?"

"Searching for something, I suppose." Joan smiled ruefully.

There was a pause, then Andrew replied, "I was too."

After tea, they stood by the window looking at the fallow ground that was to become the garden.

"The garden was to be Nancy's province," Andrew told her. "She was looking forward to planning it, but when she died, I lost heart." A look of desolation crossed his face. "For a while I even thought of selling the house." He lapsed into silence for a few moments before continuing.

"Nancy made some sketches of her ideas. Perhaps you'd like to make use of them."

He turned away and glanced out of the window. "I think it would be nice if the garden was as she wanted it, don't you?"

Though Joan agreed, she wasn't so sure. She wondered whether reminding yourself of the past was a good way of rebuilding your life.

Over the next few weeks, Joan drew up several alternative plans, taking special care to include some of Nancy's ideas. But Andrew was unable to make up his mind. He always wanted to include just that little something else which Nancy might have liked. Eventually Joan became impatient but as he'd given her no definite limit as to cost, she felt she couldn't say anything. As each plan was modified and rejected, Joan became unhappier. She had the feeling that she was planning with someone looking over her shoulder, and disapproving. She felt inhibited and unable to put her full imagination to work.

ONE morning Andrew looked at her latest design with interest as Joan explained her ideas. Then he hesitated. "I'm still not sure," he said at length.

Joan felt angry words springing to her lips.

"I'm sorry, Andrew," she said briskly. "I must have a decision. You're not my only customer and I've spent a long time on your designs, longer than I would normally do." She hesitated then spoke gently.

> ## Glen Affric
>
> WOODED isles and lupin isles,
>   Creeks on which the sunlight smiles,
> Silver birches, snow capped bens
> In Affric — fairest of the glens.
>
> Bluebells peeping 'neath the trees,
> Branches laughing in the breeze,
> Sheep and lambs in frolics gay,
> For it is the month of May.
>
> Sparkling loch of dazzling blue,
> Turning oft to purple hue,
> Winding road and shady dell,
> These I do remember well.
>
> All around — the fragrant air,
> And beauty which is ever there,
> So let's away from city's strife,
> And in thy splendour find new life.
>
> *Wilma McDonald*

"I don't think you should design with Nancy in mind. She's not here to approve or disapprove, but you are. My philosophy about gardens is that they should always give something to look forward to. Have you got something to look forward to, Andrew? Life can be barren after what you've suffered, but like a garden, life's got to be cultivated to make it grow again."

Joan broke off, realising in horror the cruel things she'd been saying.

She waited, fearful of his reaction. Andrew gazed abstractedly from the window for a moment, then turned to her.

"There's not much more to be said, is there?" he replied quietly.

Quickly Joan gathered her sketches together and turned to go.

"What I said was unforgivable," she said apologetically. "If you want the name of another landscape gardener, I'll gladly supply you with one."

"When I want another gardener I'll let you know." He smiled warmly. "Up to now you've given me every help and I'm completely satisfied with your work."

"Then you don't mind . . ." Joan began hesitantly.

"What you said," he interrupted. "No, I've been asking for something like that, and d'you know what? You were right in what you said. I've been wallowing in self pity and there's something else. Nancy would have hated having the garden turned into some kind of shrine for herself."

Joan looked at him, concern in her eyes.

"It's just the effort of starting again, isn't it? I've been through it too." Suddenly she was telling him about Iain. He listened sympathetically.

As she drove home, her mind was full of conflicting emotions. For both her and Andrew, the past was over. The last few weeks had been a soothing influence on her, easing her away from the bitterness and emptiness. But though the future beckoned, she felt just a little scared. One day, Andrew's garden was going to be completed. She wondered, what would happen then. Would she ever see him again? Joan couldn't bear the thought that she might not.

F INALLY, the day came when the last workman had gone. To celebrate, Andrew had invited her over to dinner. He'd carefully laid the table in the bay window overlooking the newly-finished garden.

"That was delicious, Andrew, thank you," Joan said as they cleared away the dishes. She laughed. "It's not very often my customers ask me out."

For the rest of the evening, they relaxed in each other's company. Finally the moment of parting arrived.

"We must meet again sometime, Joan, and see how your garden's progressing," Andrew said as she got into her car.

Sometimes, though, promises made are not easily kept because of circumstances, and that winter turned out to be a cruel one with long periods of snow, making driving very difficult through the hills.

Joan found herself with so much work on hand that she'd little time for much else. But Andrew was always in her thoughts and she found her approach to her work had become almost an automatic response. She found little of the joy in her designing that she'd felt with Andrew's garden, and when she returned to visit Strathard in the spring, it was with the thought that she'd heard nothing from Andrew all winter. She confessed her disappointment to Alison.

"Perhaps you were reading too much into the situation," Alison suggested. "After all, weren't both of you caught on the rebound as the saying goes? You both filled a gap in each other's lives when it was most needed.

"You're needing a good, long walk to clear those cobwebs, Joan. How about a walk tomorrow if the weather's nice? I'll make you sandwiches and coffee," she suggested.

Joan laughed.

"Trysting Pool again, I suppose, and more of your miracles."

EARLY next day the sound of the birds woke Joan from a restful sleep. The spring sunshine was streaming in through the curtains giving notice of a fine day.

After breakfast, walking purposefully, she set out for the pool. But by the time she'd arrived, the weather had changed. Grey clouds scudded across the sky menacingly and a keen north wind tugged at her clothing.

The pool was swollen by water from melting snows on the mountains above. Joan shivered. So much for my magic place, she thought sadly.

There were other things missing, too, she mused, such as tears and those footsteps coming across the springy turf towards her. Then suddenly everything about her life seemed to fall into perspective. The mist may have been low over the hills, but Joan's mind was clear. She must go and see Andrew right away.

He was working in the garden when she arrived.

"Hello, Joan. Alison told me you were in Strathard again." His voice was almost casual in its tone. "What d'you think of our garden?"

"Oh, Andrew, you've done wonders with it."

"I missed you, Joan," Andrew said softly. There was a tenderness in his voice that made Joan's heart leap.

"We've both suffered in our different ways," she replied, "but yesterday's not so important any more, is it?"

They looked at each other, realising the understanding between them. Gently, Andrew took hold of her hand.

"You brought me back to life, Joan."

"I'm glad." Joan smiled. "I visited the Trysting Pool today."

"Did you find any of that magic you were looking for?"

"No, Andrew, but I learned something. The only magic is the magic we make ourselves in our own hearts."

"And what about your heart, Joan? Are you willing to share it?"

Joan felt a touch of panic. She remembered how she'd shared her heart once and been hurt. Dare I risk that again, she asked herself.

"You once told me that life was like a garden," Andrew said gently. "You have to work hard to make it grow again. I'll never forget Nancy, just as you won't forget Iain." He hesitated, then said quietly, "But the future's more important, isn't it?"

Suddenly Joan knew that the hopes in her heart were going to be realised. Just as the garden was waking with the return of spring, so was her love for Andrew.

As she slipped into his arms, she knew at last she found what she'd been seeking all her life, her own very special "magic place." □

I^T was a dream mountain in miniature, clothed in icing more pristine than any snow, glistening more brightly than icicles in a morning sun. It rose from a forest of pine trees. High up on its shoulder was a tiny church with a slim spire that reached far into the sky.

On the dark back cloth, which simulated the dark void of a night sky, there gleamed countless diamond-bright pinpoint stars. And, amongst them, one shone even more brilliantly . . . the star that had guided the way to Bethlehem.

It was the most beautiful cake ever to come out of the Sangster bakehouse, Russell Sangster said and honestly believed. This was no small claim, for he was the fourth generation of Sangsters who'd baked cakes and bread for the people of Inchaber. He couldn't decide where the idea for the design had come from. Finally he gave up wondering and accepted that, from somewhere or other, an inspiration had come to him.

When the short December light waned in the narrow streets of Inchaber, and Effie Martin, who was in charge of the sales shop, turned on

nd FAR AWAY

by Margaret Cameron

the lighting in the window, Russell would occasionally steal out from his back premises for another look at his masterpiece.

He had to admit, of course, that while the cake was his, the way in which it was displayed was entirely the work of Effie and her young assistant, Maisie Syme, and Maisie's electrician boyfriend, Duncan Hewitt.

When Effie had first said she was going to devote the whole of one of their two windows to the cake, Russell had voiced his doubts. It would be a tremendous break with tradition and with Effie's usual window-dressing technique.

She had always been motivated by the belief that the greater the quantity and variety that could be displayed, the greater the possibility of activating the taste buds of window shoppers to the point of irresistibly luring them inside to buy. And past results over Christmas and New Year shopping periods had supported that theory.

But Russell Sangster gave in gracefully and consoled himself with the thought that one window would display to all and sundry that, in him, Inchaber had a baker par excellence.

Right from the start Effie had known broadly how she wanted the cake displayed and in discussion with Maisie and Duncan her idea took final shape and form. Duncan surprised her with his skill and artistic imagination. She had to admit that the final result owed a great deal to his subdued lighting and Maisie's suggestion that the foreground should be in the form of a plain to give the impression that the cake was a far-distant mountain rising from a forest of pines.

When it had been completed and they had their own private viewing, Effie was delighted.

''Now we'll see

what we'll see," she'd said. She was not disappointed. From the first day the cake was on view passers-by stopped to admire it and many customers in the shop gave their unstinted praise. And that really meant a great deal, for Inchaber folk had a tendency to be critical.

I T was late afternoon two or three days before Christmas and near to closing time. The shop was empty and Effie was thinking of locking up when she stopped and nudged Maisie and nodded towards the door, where a young man was admiring the cake.

"There he is again. It must be the third time today. And he always steps inside the doorway as if to get a different view of it . . . looking at it from all angles. I wonder who he is. I can't recall seeing him before this week."

Maisie didn't recognise the young man either but next morning as soon as she entered the shop she was able to enlighten Effie.

"I know who your mystery man is," she informed her. "Duncan was waiting for me last night when we closed and he'd seen him looking in the window. Duncan says his name is Elgin Carstairs. He's not been in Inchaber long. He's with Strang Woollen Mills and he travels abroad selling for them."

It was during the afternoon, when Elgin Carstairs walked into the shop. Maisie was busy with a customer and Effie went forward to serve him. He looked quickly at Effie and away again, as if uncertain as to what he wanted.

"I . . . could I have a packet of biscuits?"

Having got that out he half-smiled at Effie and she was conscious of vivid blue eyes in a thin brown face under a mop of black, unruly hair. She smiled back at him and momentarily, as their eyes met, Effie Martin's heart missed a beat.

He handed over the correct change and picked up the packet.

"I . . ." he began, but at that moment several customers came in. He smiled at Effie, repeated his thanks and went away.

I N a few minutes the shop was empty, and Effie, a puzzled frown in her eyes, turned to Maisie.

"I wonder what he really wanted. I'm certain it wasn't biscuits. He was just going to say something when those other folk came in."

"Maybe he came in specially to see you," Maisie said teasingly. "I'll bet it's you he's taken a fancy to and not the cake! He was going to ask you out!"

They laughed together for a moment and then Maisie voiced a question she'd often wanted to ask but had never had the courage or found the occasion to do so.

"Effie, were you ever in love with someone . . .?" She lost courage there and her voice tailed away as she watched Effie covertly.

Effie stared at her young assistant for a moment and then laughed.

"If I ever had been it could never have been kept in the dark in Inchaber, now could it?"

She laughed again, tilting back her head in a characteristic gesture and Maisie thought how attractive she really was without seeming to know it.

"Oh, yes. I was in love with someone . . . when I was eleven and he was twelve!" She paused for a moment, her thoughts winging back. "It was very serious. He was very sweet . . . and shy."

Strange, she thought, when that young man in the shop today looked at me out of those deep blue eyes how much he reminded me of that boy of those tender, innocent years of . . . how long ago?

"Well, go on . . . what happened to him?" Maisie was agog with interest and curiosity.

"I really don't know . . . his family moved away from Inchaber . . ."

A CUSTOMER came in and when she had been served Effie turned again to Maisie.

"Mind you, there was once a traveller, or should I say a rep., for a biscuit firm, who asked me to go out with him."

"And did you?"

"I did not!"

"Oh, but why? Wasn't he . . .?"

"He wasn't," Effie cut in emphatically. "He was the type who thought he had only to raise his little finger and this country bumpkin would be louping over the counter to get at him!"

A mental picture of Effie louping over the counter sent Maisie into gales of laughter.

"Would you," she asked, when she had got control of her mirth, "loup the counter if Fergus Greig asked you? Now he really fancies you. Of that I'm certain."

"That's rich!" Effie said scornfully. "The only things he's interested in are the wonders of wildlife . . . and two meat pies for his Saturday lunch!"

"Not so," Maisie defended stoutly. "When he comes in here he always hangs back until he gets you to serve him."

"Is that so? And when he comes in what does he say? 'It's a wet day' or 'It's a nice day' or some kind of a day and 'Two meat pies, please.' "

"Well, but it's a bit off-putting talking across a counter and never knowing when you'll have some old gossip listening at your shoulder! You should give him a bit of encouragement, you know . . . a little of the old 'come on.' " Maisie rolled her eyes and gave what she considered to be a seductive wiggle of her shapely figure.

"You're a little hussy," Effie said severely. "I wouldn't do that . . . even if I wanted to."

"No. I don't expect you would," Maisie conceded.

"But you don't have to do . . . well, what I was doing," Maisie burst out. "You're really very attractive, you're nice and wholesome and . . ."

"And on the shelf!" Effie cut in good-naturedly, but her young assistant's praise had brought a spot of pleasurable colour to her face. "Tell me, this eager swain you're telling me about, where has he been the past three weeks? Never once been inside the door."

"He's been busy making a television programme at the nature reserve . . . about geese, ducks, wildfowl of all kinds, based on his latest book. Duncan told me. He's keen on that sort of thing . . . wildlife, I mean."

"I didn't know Fergus wrote books. Have you read any of them?"

"Yes, I have. And you can tell from them what a gentle, genuine sort of man he is."

Effie couldn't help wondering. Sometimes she found depths in her young assistant which she had never suspected.

She looked up at the wall clock and turned to Maisie.

"If you've finished with my past and my future prospects I think we could close for the day. Three minutes . . . Oh, no!" She nodded quickly towards the door and lowered her voice. "Have you ever noticed there are certain people who never do their shopping until the final minute?"

Tapestry

WEAVE in yellow, every strand
Sunny days you held my hand,
Then I put in grey and brown,
Rainy days we spent in town.

White and blue to tell the tale
Sailing boats and wind blown sail,
Sew in red, for times when we
Watched the sun-sets o'er the sea.

Silver for the tinsel night
Met beneath the Christmas light,
Loving thoughts, my memory,
Weaves my treasured tapestry.

Iris A. Hardy.

SHE stopped short as Elgin Carstairs came almost diffidently into the shop. He had the air of someone about to be told he couldn't be served.

"Excuse me," he said. "I know I've come at the last minute when you want to get closed."

"It's quite all right," Effie assured him, smiling. "We're used to it . . . especially at this time of year. What can we do to help you?"

"I came late deliberately," he confessed. "I hoped there wouldn't be other people with you. It's about the cake in the window."

"I'm sorry," Effie told him. "It's not for sale. After New Year it's going to a party for old folk in Inchaber. Mr Sangster gives a special cake each year."

"Oh, but I don't want to buy it." He paused for a moment and then went on quickly. "It reminds me, very vividly, of a mountain I knew when I was a boy. It's in France, in the Auvergne Mountains. There's a small village at its foot. I used to go there often in the summer and sometimes at Christmas. I wondered if whoever made the cake had been there . . . if he knew the mountain."

Effie shook her head.

"No. I'm quite sure it must just be a coincidence. You went there on holiday?" she prompted, wondering whether there was more to the story.

"Yes. We lived in Paris. My father was there for some years for his firm. In the summer I used to spend a long time at the farm. I lived with the family . . . the Lefevres. I was there twice at Christmas." He paused thoughtfully for a moment and then went on. "It was seeing the cake . . . it's so like the mountain behind the farm . . . or perhaps I just imagine it to be like it. My father was transferred to Oslo and then back to London."

THERE was silence for a moment or two as Elgin remembered. "And have you been back?" Effie asked and somehow knew the answer.

He shook his head.

"No. I haven't been back." His face coloured a little and he had a look of someone found guilty of something. "I promised I'd go back . . . but I didn't."

"You promised the family you stayed with . . . the Lefevres?"

"No." There was a barely preceptible pause. "Only Annette."

"Only Annette?"

"Yes. She is the Lefevres' daughter . . . an only child. By coincidence I'm an only child too. Perhaps that was why . . . that was what made the bond between us. We were very fond of each other."

"Why didn't you go back?"

He seemed to take a long time to consider Effie's abrupt question. "I really don't know. We were very young, you see . . . just children . . ."

"Is there any reason why you shouldn't go now?"

There was much more significance in Effie's question than met the eye and he was aware of this.

"No. Except, after all this time . . . it's over sixteen years."

"I think you should keep your promise."

Maisie looked at Effie in disbelief. She seemed to have taken command of the situation and leave of her commonsense. She seemed to hold the young man's eyes riveted, compelling him to bend to her will.

"Had it been Annette who gave *you* that promise . . . " She stopped there and eyed him steadily and her gaze said all and more than she could have said in words.

Suddenly he raised his head and looked at her, decision made.

"I'll go. I'm going on holiday to my parents in London tomorrow. I've got almost two weeks. I'll go on to France."

He turned and made for the door.

"Wait," Effie called. "When you get there, will you . . . well, will you let us know?"

She wasn't very sure what it was she wanted to know but he understood.

He waved and was gone. Effie leaned back against the counter, as if she were tired, looking at Maisie with expressionless eyes.

"Gosh, isn't that terrific!" Maisie's eyes were as round as a child's with wonder. "Romance and love . . . love under a pure, peerless mountain." She realised she was quoting something she'd read somewhere but it didn't matter. It fitted her mood of the moment and the situation in which she and Effie had just been involved.

"D'you think," she asked, "he'll really go? And will she be waiting still? Or will she be married with children? And tell me, what made you play Cupid?"

"Perhaps he won't go. Perhaps he was just carried away for the moment. If he'd been thinking about it . . . if it had just been somewhere in his mind, perhaps I just triggered off his decision. Why did I say he should go? Perhaps it was for a little girl who once waited for someone who never came back."

She walked past Maisie and went to the door and turned the key.

THE days up to Hogmanay were hectic in the shop as the people of Inchaber laid in their New Year stocks. Only once or twice was the name of Elgin Carstairs mentioned between Effie and Maisie.

The last day of the old year passed in a hectic flurry of filling bags and boxes, seeing shelves and cases becoming depleted, wondering if there would be sufficient supplies to satisfy the demands of all their customers. As closing time approached, the shop was empty.

"It's like the quiet hush after a storm," Effie said, beginning to unbutton her overall. She was tired. "Well, that's it over. Another Hogmanay and another year ahead." She leaned against the counter.

"Another year of white loaves and brown loaves, buns and biscuits, cakes and cookies . . . mile upon mile of them stretching on for ever . . . wading knee deep in dough in all its fancy shapes and forms . . ."

"Effie! What on earth are you raving about?"

Effie took a deep breath and laughed a little ruefully.

"I was just thinking of what you said a wee while ago about romance and love beneath a pure and peerless mountain . . . or something like that and what will be our lot . . . or mine anyway . . . in this shop. I'll bet you, the first day we're open after New Year Alice Dunlop will come in and say, 'Effie, that brown loaf I got on Hogmanay wasn't properly risen!' How does that compare with love beneath your peerless mountain?"

They both laughed, for Effie's imitation of Alice Dunlop had been perfect. But, Maisie knew, Effie's remarks, her mood were not the result of plain grumpiness or dissatisfaction. There was something more here but at the moment she could not quite define what it was.

"It could be a lot worse, you know," Maisie said. "We might be out of a job altogether."

Her remark was cut short by the opening of the door and the entrance of a tall, spare man in tweeds. His lined tanned face spoke of one who lived most of his time out-of-doors.

"Hello, Mr Greig," Maisie said cheerfully. "You nearly got a locked door."

"I hoped I'd catch you. I was late in getting away . . ."

Whatever he was going to say was shattered by the thrusting open of the door.

"Telegram for Miss Martin."

Conscious of the eyes of the other two upon her, Effie took the envelope and murmured a word of thanks to the messenger. Slowly she opened the envelope and spread out the form on the counter.

"Goodness! Oh, my goodness! Just look . . . " Her voice rose to a squeak as she pushed the telegram towards Maisie.

Maisie read it slowly.

"Merci, Merci mille fois. Annette."

She let out something resembling a Red Indian whoop and waving the telegram above her head and danced, to the astonishment of Fergus Greig, round and round Effie Martin.

"She waited for him! She waited. It's marvellous; it's wonderful!"

They hugged each other and Fergus couldn't tell whether they were laughing or crying, perhaps they were doing a bit of both at one and the same time.

WHEN they'd quietened down and re-read the telegram the door was locked and Fergus was told what all their excitement had been about. It was only when Maisie began speculating as to whether Elgin Carstairs would bring her back with him or if he would have photographs of her to show them that Effie realised they were keeping their customer waiting.

"Sorry, we're chattering on here. What can I get for you?"

"It's quite all right. Could I have two meat pies please?"

The shop was suddenly dead silent in the anti-climax to the excitement of the previous few minutes. Only by a supreme effort of self control did Maisie prevent an outburst of hysterical laughter. She darted a sideways glance at Effie and she could have sworn there was a smile twitching about her lips.

"Yes. It so happens we just have two left."

She reached under the counter and brought out a cake box with the two pies. Well, well, Maisie thought to herself. At half past three Effie had told her the pies were finished. She must have put these two away thinking or perhaps hoping that Fergus Greig would come in.

"I know we make good pies," she heard Effie say as she put a string round the box. "But don't you ever get tired of them?"

"No." His eyes crinkled as he smiled at her. "I never eat them."

There was silence and then Effie heard herself say in a voice that didn't quite sound like her own:

"You buy them but you never eat them!"

"I give them to Judy. I only give her one at a time. You see, she wasn't well and wasn't eating and I tempted her with a bit of pie and she began eating again. I spoil her."

Maisie noticed he was smiling again as he looked at Effie, but Effie's face was totally expressionless and impersonal.

"I've had her for quite a long time, since she was a tiny puppy."

This time it was too much for Maisie. She burst into helpless laughter and tears trickled down her cheeks. At last she wiped her eyes.

But neither Fergus nor Effie was paying much attention to her and some instinct prompted her to go to the door and take a little time to turn the key. She got back to the counter in time to hear Effie, her face bright with colour, speaking to Fergus Greig.

"It's very kind of you to ask me . . . but I can't go out tonight. I've got Maisie and her boyfriend coming to my house for a meal. I promised them a return for the hard work they put in on the window decoration."

"I see. Well, perhaps another time . . ."

His voice tailed off and though he was doing his best to hide it, Maisie could see and sense his disappointment.

Say something! she willed Effie with all her might. Don't let him go like that! It seemed to her like an eternity before Effie spoke again.

"But if you'd care to come and join us. It won't be haute cuisine, you know. But, on the other hand, it won't be pies!"

"I'd like to, very much. Even if it were pies!"

Effie scribbled on a white paper bag and pushed it over the counter to him.

"That's my address. Say, in an hour's time."

He went off, and a bemused Maisie, who felt the whole day was beginning to get a bit out of hand, locked the door behind him. She went back to Effie and they laughed again, this time for no particular reason except that somehow there seemed to be a lot of happiness around.

They put on their coats and extinguished the lights except for those in the windows and went out to find Duncan Hewitt waiting for Maisie. For a minute they all stood looking at their little shining mountain, not saying anything but savouring a moment of satisfaction with their small creation.

Effie left them after reminding them not to be late for their meal and walked off briskly, almost jauntily, Maisie thought.

"White loaves, brown loaves, buns and biscuits . . . mile upon mile of them . . . stretching on for ever!" Maisie recited to herself as she watched Effie's figure receding.

"What are you muttering about?" Duncan asked, peering down at her.

"Oh, it's just something I heard . . . a quotation or something." She laughed up at him. "It doesn't mean anything. Not now. Oh, no, not now!" □

From being a small fishing and market town of 3000 people, Thurso was thrust into the Atomic Age with the building of the nearby Dounreay Fast Reactor in the 1950s and now has a population of around 9000 with burgeoning housing schemes to the west and east of the town. Situated on the North Coast of Caithness, looking across Thurso Bay to the towering cliffs of Dunnet Head and over the Pentland Firth to the Orkneys beyond, the town has strong Viking connections, which are still evident to this day; not least in the local pronunciation of the name, "Thursa," meaning river of the god Thor.

THURSO: J CAMPBELL KERR

A Lot Of Thinking To Do

By Elspeth Rae

GILLY CARSON looked at her watch and sighed. 7.35 already! And she had to meet Peter at eight. Usually, her young sister's gym class came out right on time.

What on earth could be holding them up this evening?

Gilly began strolling slowly across the deserted school playground towards the door of the hall, where the Craigbridge Gymnastics Club met on Fridays. It was already dusk on this windy, March evening, and the hall was lit up.

Once the evenings were lighter, twelve-year-old Kirsty and her friends could walk home on their own. Until then, though, Gilly had willingly offered to escort them.

Gilly was almost at the hall door when it suddenly flew open, and a young man in a blue tracksuit shot out and hurried over to a large, green van.

Within seconds, the van had been reversed right up to the door and a crowd of girls in black leotards started loading it up. Gym mats, hoops, bean-bags — they were all quickly stowed away.

"You've certainly got them well organised!" Gilly smiled to the young instructor, who had just caught sight of her.

Colin Hood grinned.

"Yes," he said. "I rule them with a rod of iron. You've no idea!"

"They seem to enjoy it anyway," Gilly commented, as the happy girls started to troop past them and away.

The young man nodded.

"I could do with a bit of help, though," he remarked. "I have twenty of them coming now. So if you ever have a free Friday evening . . ."

"I'll remember!" Gilly smiled, turning to leave as red-haired Kirsty and her two friends, Ruth and Susan, finally emerged from the hall.

GILLY saw right away that there was something troubling Kirsty, for her young sister was chattering much too loudly and brightly to the other girls, as they made their way home across the recreation ground.

Kirsty always adopted the same manner if she had been hurt or disappointed in any way. She was a proud little soul and hated to let the world see she was feeling bad. Only when Ruth and Susan had left them, though, did Gilly put a hand on her young sister's shoulder.

"Something wrong, Kirsty?" she enquired gently.

"No! Of course not!" The younger girl began, tossing back her auburn curls. Then, to Gilly's amazement and horror, she suddenly stopped dead and burst into tears.

"Kirsty!" Gilly's arm was encircling her young sister in a flash. "Come on, love! It can't be as bad as that," Gilly whispered, handing Kirsty a tissue to wipe her eyes. "What's it all about? Can you tell me?"

"He's put me out of the team," Kirsty managed to tell Gilly between sobs. "Colin's put me out of the team for next week's regional tournament."

"Oh, no!" Gilly's brown eyes sparkled with indignation. "After the way you've been practising, too! I thought you were in top form when I watched you last night."

"It's not because of my gymnastics," Kirsty explained, finally calming down and taking her sister's arm as they walked on. "It's because I was wearing my purple leotard tonight and not my black club leotard. He says if I can't obey the rules about dress, he can't rely on me."

"But that's unfair!" There were two bright spots of colour on Gilly's cheeks. "Didn't you explain that Mum had forgotten to wash your club leotard?"

"I didn't have a chance." Kirsty gulped. "Colin doesn't let you explain anything. He's like a sergeant-major! If I wasn't so keen on gymnastics I'd leave his rotten old club!"

Gilly was still seething inwardly twenty minutes later when she left the bus at the corner of Market Street. Peter Fraser, who had been leaning against the wall of the bank, came forward to greet her.

"Sorry I'm late, darling!" Gilly apologised and as they set off along the brightly-lit street, she spilled out her indignation about young Kirsty.

"It certainly seems a bit rough," Peter agreed, as he guided the pretty young woman into the Golden Bell Coffee Bar. "But if this Colin Hood runs the club and makes the rules, what can you do about it?"

Gilly's brown eyes darkened as she sat down opposite Peter.

"I can tell him what I think of his rules!" she retorted. "He helps his father on his fruit and vegetable stall in the Saturday market, so I'll have a word with him tomorrow!"

"Are you serious?" Peter Fraser's grey eyes were uneasy as he looked across at his girlfriend. "Because if you are, I don't think that's a very good idea, Gilly. It will only cause unpleasantness and make things difficult for Kirsty."

"Kirsty couldn't be any more miserable than she is this evening?" Gilly exploded. "And it'll make me feel a lot better if I give Colin Hood a piece of my mind!"

"Well, I expect you'll have calmed down by tomorrow," Peter remarked, his eyes twinkling at Gilly over his coffee cup, "so let's change the subject. Have you decided yet what you're going to wear tomorrow evening?"

"Yes, I have," she said, enthusiastically. "I'll wear my red dress. But I must buy some new shoes to go with it. Will you meet me tomorrow afternoon and help me choose?"

Peter gave an exaggerated groan.

"I suppose I'll have to." He sighed. "After all, it is my cousin's engagement party that's putting you to all this expense."

"I wanted new shoes anyway," Gilly told him, then added quietly, "and it's not as though I'm saving for anything else."

Peter flushed slightly, then quickly began to describe an amusing incident that had taken place that afternoon at work.

IT was always the same, Gilly thought ruefully, as she listened to Peter's story. She and Peter had been going out together for two years now, and he was closer to her than anyone in the world. Yet the slightest allusion to marriage plans and Peter shied away like a startled pony!

During the past year, two of his colleagues in the post office had become engaged, and on each occasion Peter had made the same comment.

"It's crazy! Fancy getting married on a salary like ours!"

And Peter's slim, smartly-dressed mother was obviously of the same opinion.

"Imagine starting married life in a tiny, rented flat!" she had exclaimed to Gilly. "You'd think they could have waited until they had passed all their exams and could have afforded somewhere half-decent. It must be such a disappointment for their parents!"

Gilly had been too polite to disagree with Peter's mother. But recently, she had become increasingly concerned about Peter's own attitude. From the way he talked it would be years before he would feel himself in a position to settle down. And, much as she loved Peter, Gilly had no desire to drift along with him for an indefinite period.

"Wake up, dreamy!" Peter gave Gilly a playful tap on the cheek to jerk her out of her reverie. "I was asking whether you wanted me to call for you tomorrow evening," he went on, "or shall we meet outside the hotel?"

"Oh, let's meet at the hotel." Gilly smiled as they rose to leave. "It would be silly for you to come trailing over to our place. I can catch a bus at the corner that takes me all the way there."

Gilly was homeward-bound and settled into the corner seat of the bus before young Kirsty's disappointment returned to her thoughts.

And I'll tackle Colin Hood tomorrow, she decided as she suddenly recalled her young sister's tear-stained face. I don't care what Peter thinks!

K IRSTY was in bed when Gilly arrived home, so Gilly could freely discuss her young sister's disappointment with her parents. To her surprise, her mother proffered much the same advice as Peter had.

"I wouldn't interfere, Gilly!" Mrs Carson said firmly as she handed mugs of hot chocolate to her husband and her daughter. "Kirsty's at an age when problems like this are best left to blow over. She'll shed a few tears tonight, but by tomorrow things won't look nearly so black to her."

"But it wasn't Kirsty's fault, Mum!" Gilly answered hotly. "It's all quite unfair."

"Then she should have spoken up for herself!" Jim Carson looked over his spectacles at his elder daughter. "There must surely have been an opportunity for her to explain. You can't fight Kirsty's battles for her for ever, Gilly!"

"I don't intend to!" Gilly retorted, looking at both her parents in exasperation. "I just want to put that high-handed Colin Hood in his place and show him he can't get off with bullying my young sister! Kirsty was broken-hearted this evening — you should have seen her!"

As Gilly ran upstairs to bed a few minutes later, Liz Carson looked across at her husband and shook her head.

"She's always been over-protective where Kirsty's concerned," she remarked.

"Mmm." Jim Carson smiled wryly as he rose to wind the clock. "And she's maybe a wee bit bossy, too," he remarked. "I suppose it comes of her being a super-efficient private secretary. It's time young Peter married the girl and kept her in order."

"Yes! I wish he'd get a move on!" Liz Carson sighed again, as she ushered her husband out of the sitting-room and switched off the light. "Peter's a real nice lad. But I sometimes wonder how long Gilly will wait for him. Her patience will run out sometime!"

I T was Peter's patience that almost ran out the following afternoon, though. For by five o'clock the young couple had visited every shoe shop in Craigbridge at least twice.

The town hall clock was striking the hour when Gilly finally settled on a pair of black sandals, a much more expensive pair than she had originally intended to buy.

In fact, having paid for them, she discovered she had a solitary five-pence piece left in her purse.

As they left the shop, Gilly put her hand on Peter's arm, intending to ask him for a loan of her bus-fare home.

Then she suddenly came to a halt. Just in front of them was the Hoods' fruit and vegetable stall, and Colin Hood himself, whistling cheerfully, was packing the few remaining vegetables into crates.

"There he is! Come on, Peter! Let's go and have a word with him now!" Gilly's mouth was set in a firm line as she tugged Peter's arm impatiently.

"No! I will not!" Peter exclaimed in a horrified tone. "Don't be so silly! You're acting like a child, Gilly! You can't start a quarrel in the street. What will people think?"

Gilly swung round to face her boyfriend, cheeks scarlet.

"I don't really care!" she retorted. "And the trouble with you, Peter Fraser, is that you care too much! You spend your life worrying about what people will think!"

LEAVING Peter's side, Gilly marched over to the stall just as Colin Hood finished stacking his pile of crates. The young man beamed when he caught sight of her.

"I know!" he exclaimed. "You're going to come and help on Friday evenings! Did Kirsty talk you into it?"

"As a matter of fact," Gilly said curtly, "Kirsty was too upset to talk at all yesterday evening, Mr Hood! I don't know if you realised how hard she had worked for next week's tournament!"

Colin Hood nodded, reddening slightly.

"I was really sorry about having to drop her," he admitted, "but rules are rules. And if I don't keep the girls up to the mark about their dress, their gymnastic work becomes careless, too."

"Well you might at least have let the poor child explain why she didn't have her club leotard!" Gilly went on hotly. "It was Mum who had forgotten to wash it. You can hardly blame Kirsty for that!"

"Why didn't she say so, then?" Colin Hood asked, eyes flashing.

"Because I gather you rant and rave at them like a sergeant-major!" Gilly replied angrily. "It seems a funny way to treat a lot of little girls, I must say!"

"Perhaps you should come and run the club, then! If you know so much about dealing with little girls!" Colin Hood's face was scarlet, as he moved away angrily to start loading crates into his father's van.

Gilly wheeled round to speak to Peter. But her boyfriend had gone, and she could see no sign of him anywhere along the street. Gilly bit her lip. Honestly! It was too much!

Surely Peter could have waited for her, even though he hadn't wanted her to speak to Colin Hood about Kirsty!

Then another thought struck Gilly. She hadn't enough money for her bus-fare home! She placed the parcel containing her sandals on the stall, and began to search furiously through her bag.

No, it was no good! She had only the five pence that was in her purse. She would either have to walk home, or go through the embarrassing procedure of giving her name and address to the bus driver.

In the end, Gilly decided to walk. It was six o'clock by the time she arrived home, exhausted and with a blister on her heel.

Then, as she opened the front-door, she suddenly realised that she had lost something. It was the parcel containing her new sandals! Frantically racking her mind, she remembered where she had left it — on Colin Hood's fruit and vegetable stall!

* * * *

Peter's mother answered the phone when Gilly rang at six-thirty.

"He's still in the bath, dear," Mrs Fraser said. "He's going to have a dreadful rush. He's not long in. Can I give him a message?"

"Just tell him I won't be able to make it tonight, Mrs Fraser," Gilly said tightly. "I should think he'll understand why."

"Oh, what a pity! I am sorry!" Mrs Fraser said kindly. "I hope there's nothing wrong?" she added.

"No, nothing serious," Gilly replied awkwardly, before she wished Mrs Fraser goodbye, and hung up.

Gilly's mother, mixing a cake in the kitchen, frowned as Gilly poked her head in at the door.

"You surely could have found another pair of shoes to wear, dear!" she said. "It seems awful to let Peter down for a trifle like that."

"It's not just that, Mum," Gilly said quietly. "I've suddenly decided I have a lot of thinking to do, and that I'd better start tonight."

She hurried upstairs, summoning up a smile for Kirsty, who came dashing

HOUSEHOLD PETS

*P*ADDY *the cat; Charlie the dog.*
Resident live-stock, taken for granted.

Little noted when the house was a-stir.

Girls with their friends in; Andy his cronies.

What change has the twelve-month brought!

With Cathie in Leeds, Ella to nurse in London, and Andy gone to the Navy.

Now her husband departed; Far East on business,

The thing that she dreaded – Anne was alone!

Save for Paddy the cat and Charlie the dog.

Pets no more but members of the household.

To speak to, fuss over and answer their needs.

Three now for meals and three in the fireside circle.

"How can I feel lonely?" asked Anne,

"When there's three of us still in the house!"

Rev. T. R. S. Campbell.

down on her way out to the cinema. She seemed to have cheered up just as her mother had predicted.

Once in the privacy of her room, Gilly flung herself face down on her bed. After all, perhaps the tiff with Peter had been a good thing, she reflected sadly.

She couldn't shut her eyes to the problem any longer. She had to decide whether she wanted to continue a romance with Peter with no prospect of an engagement or marriage in sight, or whether she ought to break free and perhaps meet someone else who wanted the same things out of life as she did.

It had been Gilly's frequent trips to the post office for Mr Henderson, her boss, that had brought Peter Fraser into her life.

She had been attracted to the quietly-spoken counter clerk with the clear, grey eyes right from the start. Soon they had got into the habit of chatting if the post office wasn't too busy.

Then, one spring day, Peter had asked Gilly rather shyly if she would like to come to the cinema with him. She had accepted with an alacrity that had made the young man's face light up.

That had been two years ago, and they had been going out together regularly ever since. From the beginning they had got on remarkably well.

They had the same sense of humour and a similar taste in entertainment. They both played tennis, though not very seriously, and they enjoyed long country walks.

Peter lived with his parents in a flat on the other side of town from the Carsons. He had invited Gilly home for tea shortly after they had started going out together.

Gilly had taken to Peter's parents right away, but the longer she knew them, the more she could see how much they enjoyed creating a good impression.

It seemed they furnished their home more for effect than for their own comfort. And Peter, it seemed, had inherited their attitude. He was determined that his own first home would be a place to show off proudly to friends and relations.

And for this reason he was willing to wait for years before he married.

Yes, indeed! What other people thought was obviously so important to Peter that he could walk off and leave Gilly without a word, as he had done that afternoon!

Well, it wouldn't do, Gilly thought bitterly! Peter obviously meant more to her than she did to him and if this was the case, she was bound to get badly hurt sooner or later. There was only one solution, and that was to break with him.

Having finally come to her decision, Gilly buried her head in her pillow and began to weep as though her heart would break.

IN an effort to make herself feel better, Gilly washed her hair the following morning as soon as she got up. She was sitting at her bedroom mirror drying it, when she heard the penetrating jangle of the front door bell.

A minute later, her bedroom door burst open and Kirsty bounded in, green eyes dancing excitedly. She plumped an oblong parcel on Gilly's lap.

"Cinderella's slippers!" The auburn-haired girl giggled. "Prince Charming's just delivered them. He's down in the sitting-room waiting to see you."

With a sigh, Gilly started downstairs. She didn't feel much like facing anyone this morning. Far less a young man with whom she was barely on speaking terms.

"Peter!" Gilly exclaimed incredulously. For it was her boyfriend who had swung round from the window to face her, his grey eyes anxious. "What on earth are you doing here?" Gilly asked in bewilderment. "How did you come to have my sandals?"

Peter put his hand up protestingly.

"One question at a time!" He laughed, coming forward to kiss her on the forehead. "Colin Hood gave me your sandals yesterday," he explained, "after you'd done your disappearing act."

"But it was you who disappeared!" Gilly remonstrated.

"Rubbish!" Peter retorted, his eyes dancing. "All I did was pop into the newsagent's while you were ranting at poor Colin. And when I came back you'd gone. I asked Colin Hood about you, and he asked me to pass on your sandals and an apology as well. So here I am."

"Oh, Peter!" Gilly looked miserably down at the carpet. "I thought you'd deserted me. And on top of that I had to walk home, because I didn't have my fare. I'm sorry I let you down last night . . ."

NO, Gilly!" Peter gripped the girl by the shoulders. "Don't apologise. You were quite right in what you said to me in the market. I have always worried too much about what other people think. But it wasn't until last night at my cousin's party that the truth suddenly hit me."

"Oh, Peter!" Gilly put her arms around the young man and held him close.

"In the middle of all that noise and hilarity, I realised I might have lost you, Gill! Then I looked at my cousin sitting so happily beside her fiance and I knew what a fool I'd been." He sighed.

"I realised then that it was only you who mattered. Not a smart house, or a car, or even what my parents think. Just you, Gilly Carson! So . . . will you marry me? Please? Just as soon as we can arrange it?"

"Yes! Yes — of course I will, silly!" Gilly whispered, with a little hiccup that might have been a sob.

A tap at the sitting-room door made them both swing round. Kirsty was standing there, her face radiant.

"Have you told Gilly the news, Peter?" she asked breathlessly.

"Not yet, love." Peter laughed. Then he turned to Gilly. "Colin Hood asked me to tell Kirsty she was back in the tournament team," he explained.

"Fantastic!" Gilly danced forward to grab her young sister round the waist. "And what about our news, Kirsty Carson?" she went on gaily. "Peter and I are going to be married soon."

"And high time, too!" Kirsty retorted with a toss of her auburn curls. "I thought I was never going to be a bridesmaid!"

"And so say all of us!" Liz Carson, breathed, eyes twinkling, as she tiptoed down the last few stairs, and hurried through the hall to the kitchen to tell her husband the good news. □

by
Jean
McDougall

An Evening For Romance

D O you think we're doing the right thing?'' Mandy asked the girl
opposite her in the compartment. She'd been asking that question in various forms throughout the journey to Easterduns, but
Irene showed no impatience.

"We'll soon find out," she answered lightly, laying aside the
magazine she had been reading, and sending a comforting smile in her
sister's direction.

Mandy had been through so much in her short life — the motor
accident, having to nurse her young husband for many months as a result
of his injuries, and finally widowhood — that Irene couldn't blame her
for viewing every step of the future with misgiving.

"At least we'll be together," she added warmly.

"Thank goodness for that. I don't know what I'd have done without
you, Irene, when Dennis was lying so ill."

"Look, dear, there's our first glimpse of the sea," Irene interposed,
trying to steer the younger girl away from sorrowful memories.
"Remember how we used to vie with each other at holiday times as to
who would see it first?"

An Evening For Romance

A S regular as clockwork, the family had travelled eastwards to stay in Aunt Clara's house and the tradition had continued even after their parents had died, though now and again they'd varied it by taking holidays abroad.

A busy woman, she had taken over the operation of the village's general store after her husband died, and ran it successfully with the help of an old family friend, widower Angus Watson.

It had come as something of a surprise that, on her death, Clara hadn't left the business to Angus, but to her two nieces.

The sisters had talked over accepting their inheritance long and earnestly and finally they'd decided to return to where they had spent so many happy holidays with the intention of coaxing Angus into remaining at his post behind the counter. At his age, after all, finding another post would be a near impossibility.

Irene had had a good job as private secretary to the chairman of a components factory. But, unfortunately, it had fallen on bad times like so many other small businesses and the entire staff had been made redundant.

Before she'd found a new job the news had come of Aunt Clara's passing, sudden and peaceful just as she wanted it, and the business that was now hers and Mandy's.

"Do you suppose Paul Moore will be around?" she asked Irene wistfully, and again the older girl felt a stirring of anxious protectiveness. Mandy mustn't be hurt again, not if she had anything to do with it.

"He's probably married by now with a family of youngsters." She laughed, hoping devoutly the younger girl wasn't building on old, burnt-out romances.

There had been a time when Mandy and Paul had fallen for each other in a big way, mooning around the little holiday resort, or drifting happily on the surface of the smooth bay in one of his father's boats.

Then, after a silly tiff, Mandy had perversely turned to the latest visitor, handsome Dennis Strong who loved fast cars and generally having a good time.

Irene had felt sorry for Paul, knowing how rejected and unhappy he must be, but sure that her sister would come to her senses and realise who was the better man.

Instead, though, Mandy and Dennis's friendship had turned to romance and soon they were married. It had been a highly-successful marriage, brought to an abrupt end only because of his passion for dangerously-high speeds.

"I suppose you're right." Mandy was collecting her things together as they neared the station. "It's a big mistake to think everyone will be exactly as they were years ago when you make up your mind to look them up again."

"I know he'll be delighted to see you again," Irene said softly. She had seen the letter Paul had sent her sister after her husband's death. It had been written with care to cause no hurt and give the maximum of comfort under the sad circumstances.

It was the kind of letter that only a deeply-thoughtful, kindly man could have written, and she knew Mandy had read and wept over it many times, treasuring it above the many others that had arrived.

S ENSIBLY, they had arranged rooms for themselves in Easterduns Hotel. Aunt Clara's house was also theirs, but it would be cold and empty now, and they couldn't face the thought of opening it up after their long journey. Time enough when they had dined and rested and said hello to Angus again.

Luckily, the hotel wasn't far away, but if they'd expected it to be unchanged, they were in for a big surprise. The proprietor had extended it to include what looked like a small ballroom and additional bedrooms.

"Goodness!" Mandy was impressed. "This looks all right, doesn't it, Irene?"

"Glad you approve." A dark, rather stockily-built man appeared from behind her.

Mandy's fair skin went a bit pinker, and Irene couldn't help smiling at her discomfiture.

"You could have said it looked ghastly," Les Forrest continued gravely, but deep in the grey eyes Irene thought she spotted a twinkle. "Are you ladies looking for accommodation?"

"We've got bookings," Irene told him. "Mrs Strong and Miss Kirkwood."

"Good. Here are your keys, and I'll have the cases brought up to you. You'll be dining here, I expect, and tonight we've a band coming along, so if you feel like dancing . . ."

Upstairs the rooms were pleasantly furnished and the bed linen immaculate. There were extension phones and the shared bathroom had piping-hot water.

M ANDY was the first to go for a bath. While she was in the bath-room the phone rang. Irene answered it.

"It's yourself, Paul!" she exclaimed delightedly. "How have you been?"

"Mandy? How are you? I'm fine."

"It's Irene," she told him, smiling. "Or don't you remember me?"

"Of course I do. Sorry about the mistake. Your voices always sounded so alike."

"Yes. Mandy's having a refreshing bath right now, but I'm sure she'll be here in a minute for a word with you, Paul. It's been a long, long time."

"You've said it. I hear you're the big-time executive now."

She chuckled at that.

"You heard wrong then. All I am is the big-time secretary — retired. Well, not exactly retired, but certainly redundant. How about yourself?"

"Oh, still in boat building and boat hiring. My father doesn't do any heavy work now, since his heart attack, but we've a good team of workers. Everyone pulls together."

He would be a fair boss, she was thinking, as the dividing door opened
and her sister wafted in, bringing a pleasant fragrance of expensive talc
and bath oil with her. Irene handed her the phone.

"Paul!" she exclaimed delightedly. "Oh, Paul! How marvellous to
hear your voice again. Tell me all about yourself and what you've been
doing."

I RENE tiptoed away to run her bath. If only one could foresee the
future, she mused, just to arm oneself against any possible hurt or
injury, but of course one couldn't.

She reminded herself that her sister was a grown woman now, and
should be well able to look out for herself, but she couldn't help dreading
the possibility of her being hurt again.

Paul had known they were on their way, so he was probably simply
doing the friendly thing, ringing up to welcome them to his home
town and offering to help with things in any way he could.

At holiday times he had always been like a big brother to them,
teasing and tormenting, affectionately hugging, and now and again
bawling them out for some misdemeanour. She remembered at least one
time when she had earned a rush of his short temper.

It had been a beautiful day, the glass-like surface of the water
reflecting houses and hills so that she'd seemed to be living a happy
dream.

One of the Moore Company's boats was lying up at a jetty and so
she'd clambered aboard, slipped the rope knot and pushed off towards
the middle of the bay. She'd been about to lie back and let herself drift
aimlessly, when she'd seen water seeping in under her feet, and seconds
later she was bailing frantically to stay afloat.

In hardly any time, though to her it seemed an eternity, he was
skimming over the water in a motor boat, closing in and shouting angry
directions to her to secure the rope he threw to bring in the boat.

Then he was hauling her aboard and she didn't need to look at his face
to realise how angry he was at this piece of crass stupidity.

"I'm . . . so sorry."

"And so you ought to be. Of all the foolhardy things to do. Surely
you know this is a boat repair yard. To take a boat without permission
isn't just thoughtless, it's downright crazy. If I ever catch you doing
such a thing again . . ."

He forgave her in time, later even jokingly asking if she had hi-jacked
any good boats recently.

M ANDY was just putting the phone down when Irene emerged from
the bath, and she gave her a happy smile.

"Paul's dropping by tonight. Said he'd have dinner with us."
Irene picked up her hairbrush thoughtfully.

"Would you mind very much if I skip the meal?" she asked as she
started to brush her hair.

"No — but why?" Mandy asked in surprise.

"I'm not all that hungry. I think I'll let you two mull over old times together, and I'll take a walk down by Aunt Clara's house. I might even drop in to see old Angus. Don't worry. I'll be back in plenty of time to say hello to Paul."

"Well, if you're sure that's what you want to do. But Paul's sure to feel he's doing you out of your dinner."

"Nonsense! If you explain properly, he won't give it another thought."

L EAVING the hotel, Irene strolled along the familiar main street, noticing the changes, but Aunt Clara's shop looked as it always had done, a fascinating window through which generations of children had peered wide eyed.

The same old bead curtains hung at the back, partially obscuring the interior. So often in the past had she seen Aunt Clara's smiling face peering through the curtains that she imagined she could see her now, beaming happily at having her two "chickens" back under her wing.

Tears sprang to her eyes and she was about to turn away, but someone was inside and had spotted her.

Through the door, to the accompaniment of the high, pinging bell, came the stoutish figure of Angus Watson, hastily adjusting his distance glasses the better to see her.

When You're Near

THE feeling that I have for you
    Is softer than a candle's glow,
And when you are away, my love,
    It waits uncertain, flickering low,
But leaps and dances when you're there,
    Rekindled by the love we share.

The feeling that I have for you
    Is sweet as any melody,
And when you are not by my side
    It has a low and haunting key,
But soars with joy when you are near
Because, my love, you are so dear.

Sylvia Hart.

"Ah, Irene! Good to see you, love."

"Angus! You look just as you always did. Not a day older."

"And certainly no younger. But don't stand out here, girl, come away in."

She followed him inside.

"Aren't you thinking of closing? I suspect you work far longer than you need in the old shop. You always did."

"I'd be lost without it, but I'm real glad you and your sister are coming in to help with the paper work. That blessed V.A.T. drives me mad."

Irene watched Angus brew a cup of coffee on the gas ring at the back.

"Mandy and I can't quite understand why you weren't left the shop, Angus," she began gently. "We always thought . . ."

"Och, your aunt was wiser than the pair of you," Angus interrupted her. "She knew the responsibility would drive me up the wall. No, I'm not executive material, as they call it nowadays. All I ever wanted to do was work behind the counter, have a crack with the customers, a wee joke or two, and drop the takings through the bank's safety deposit at night."

He brought the coffee over to the table.

"Have you heard from Paul yet?" Angus asked as they shared coffee and biscuits together.

"Yes. He phoned, and he's probably having dinner with my sister right this minute." She was aware of the keen glance he shot her and changed the subject quickly.

"Wouldn't you like to come back to the hotel and say hello to Mandy?"

He shook his head firmly.

"Haven't been in the place for years. They tell me it's posh now. Anyway, I'll be seeing you both in the shop soon, and I've got things to do at home."

"Just as you like, Angus. See you tomorrow, and we can have another talk about things."

A few couples were strolling along the promenade in the still-bright evening, but the wind was chill now and she was conscious of the fact she'd walked out of the hotel after a hot bath without a coat.

Serve me right if I come down with a cold, she thought. Of all the daft things to do!

In her time she'd done a few daft things — like taking out an unseaworthy boat, like falling in love with her sister's boyfriend.

She caught her breath then, for it was the first time she'd ever admitted to herself how she had really felt about Paul. Maybe all those years it had been glossed over and forgotten, but one look from Angus's eyes had brought home to her the depth of her true feelings.

But all that was years ago, and nothing had really changed. It was Mandy that Paul had telephoned this evening, and it was Mandy he was dining with.

Well, even though a threesome could often seem a bit crowded, it was time she was heading back to the hotel, otherwise Mandy might imagine she'd fallen off the jetty, or something. On the other hand, these two might be so wrapped up in each other, they might not even have noticed her absence.

A MOMENT later, however, she spotted Mandy and Paul walking along the promenade together, Mandy well wrapped against the wind, Paul scanning the horizon as though afraid Irene might have taken off in one of his boats again. Smiling, Irene waved and hurried towards them.

"What are you doing out without a coat, Irene? You must be frozen." Paul's voice sounded more accusing than welcoming. Before she could protest, he had whipped off his windcheater, and was unceremoniously bundling her into it.

"Still as bossy as ever," she remarked, once she got her breath back.

"Still as stubborn as ever," he retorted, then placing himself in the middle, he took a girl on either side under his arms and walked along at a spanking pace.

"I don't know about you two, but I'm hungry, and that's a smashing menu Les Forrest has laid on at the hotel. It's be a shame to pass it up."

"Haven't you eaten yet?" Irene asked in surprise.

Mandy looked round at her sister.

"No — thanks to you stravaiging off like that. Paul wouldn't hear of us dining without you — so there you are."

THE dancing was already in full swing when they reached the hotel but he steered them purposefully to the dining-room, which by now was emptying fast in favour of the rhythmic sounds from the ballroom.

Under the lights, Irene could see that Paul had changed over the years. He no longer looked quite so boyish and he had one or two grey hairs now, but he looked suntanned and healthy from his outdoor life.

Watching him listening attentively to some story her sister was telling, Irene could see the old attraction between them still existed. But, she mused, it was kind of him to wait until she'd joined them before dining.

Their meal over, they rose to join the dancers. Irene decided that after a short while she would plead unpacking to be done, or say she wanted to wash her hair.

However, before she'd had a chance to speak, Les Forrest joined them. It was apparent he and Paul were old friends but, nevertheless, Irene felt a bit irritated by him making up the foursome. Now she could hardly excuse herself without appearing rude.

Les turned out to be an excellent dancer, however, and Irene found her tiredness receding in the swing of the music, and that she was beginning to enjoy the evening. He was a good conversationalist, too, and his amusing remarks kept her entertained.

Then it was time to change partners and as Paul led her on to the dance floor she had to remind herself he was Mandy's friend, always had been, always would be.

Still, it was intriguing how the years rolled away as though they had never been. He was the same unaffected, outspoken Paul, as his first remark showed.

"You're as stiff as a board, Irene. You never used to be. What's wrong?"

"Not a thing. You've just forgotten what a rotten dancer I was — still am."

"I remember everything about you, Irene, and you can take it from me, that wasn't one of your faults."

Startled, she pulled away to look up at him, but there was no teasing in his face, only a faint sadness.

"I often wanted to get in touch," he continued, "but when I heard you were practically engaged, I realised I'd waited too long."

Another of the daft things she'd done was to take up with one of the company's junior executives. At one stage, she had even contemplated marriage, and of course Aunt Clara had heard all about it. But the affair had petered out. If only Paul had got in touch. But then, what about Mandy?

THOUGH the music was swinging on, by common consent they dropped out to sit at one of the small tables in a corner.

"I got over the disappointment about Mandy years ago," he said frankly. "Once she and Dennis married, that was that, as far as I was concerned."

He shrugged expressively.

"As far as girls are concerned, I appear to be an all-time champion loser."

"That I don't believe," Irene said quietly. "And you've overlooked one thing — the situation with Mandy's different now. She's a free agent again."

He caught her hand.

"You wouldn't be trying to farm me off, would you?"

"No, Paul. Don't be an idiot." The touch of his hand was sending shivers down her spine, but she continued doggedly.

"It's just that I couldn't bear Mandy being hurt all over again. She's been through so much."

"I know." He inclined his head to survey the whirling throng.

Suddenly he laughed. Irene looked at him indignantly.

"So you were just joking," she said angrily. "I hope you find it all highly amusing."

"Don't lose your cool, lass. Take a look at that sister of yours that you protect like some old mother hen."

Mandy was dancing, held closely by Les Forrest, who was whispering in her ear. She was laughing up at him.

"It could be a pointer to the future," Paul said gently. "She could do a lot worse than Les Forrest. I know him well and, believe me, you couldn't meet a nicer fellow."

But Irene couldn't agree with him. After all, she'd met a nicer fellow all these years ago, and miraculously he was now in love with her and not Mandy. That could be another pointer to the future.

Suddenly her whole being was suffused with happiness.

Dear Aunt Clara had made sure she came back to Easterduns by leaving the shop to herself and Mandy. She had a sudden thought of the keen look Angus had shot her when Paul's name had come up in the conversation. No doubt tomorrow when he learned how things had turned out, his eyes would glisten behind his glasses.

"Hello, you two." Mandy had returned to flop in a chair while Les went in search of iced drinks. "I'm having the most wonderful time. How about you?"

"Wonderful!" Paul and Irene said together.

With perfect timing the band struck up "I'm In Love With A Wonderful Guy."

"Why don't you two give it a whirl?" Mandy suggested. "I'll wait here for Les." □

THE STOWAWAY

"O F course I'll stay at the cottage for a couple of weeks," Philippa said. "We break up on Thursday, and anything's a welcome change from primary kids."

"It *could* be lonely . . . " Aunt Rhona began. "There isn't much life in Leighpuddle. Not for a young girl like you."

"I'm twenty-four," her niece reminded her. "You do forget, don't you? And you can't possibly go yourself while Uncle is so poorly. Let me do this to help you."

"You won't brood . . . all on your own in a country village?"

"You mean because of Richard? No, I promise I won't brood. I've got over him at last. At least I think I have. I don't think about him all the time now."

"How long do the thatchers expect to be working?"

"It depends on the weather, of course, but three weeks at the most."

"Then stop worrying. I'll enjoy myself. I'll relax, try to collect a tan, and catch up on my reading; and, I shall have nothing whatever to do with *men!*"

A suspicion of a smile flitted over Aunt Rhona's face.

"You're a good girl, Philippa," she said. "I don't know what we should have done without you over the past few years."

"I don't know what I'd have done without you, with my parents trotting round the oil countries so much of the time."

"Talking of men," her aunt said suddenly, "I forgot to tell you that Fred's nephew, Rod, will be coming in to decorate the bathroom while you are there. The ceiling's marked where the old thatch leaked."

"I shouldn't imagine Fred's nephew would be a threat to my peace of mind, should you?" Philippa observed. "Particularly if he's anything like Fred."

T HE thatchers were well into the job when Philippa reached the cottage.

"We 'ave to take advantage of the weather, ye see, miss," the foreman explained in his broad Dorset dialect. "This sort of weather is too good to last."

She spent the first day blissfully relaxing in the overgrown orchard at the back of the cottage, watching the men working on the roof. It was an idyllic spot, not too far from the sea, and with a faint line of the Purbeck Hills just within view.

The next morning, which was still warm and sunny, she put on a cotton frock and walked over the little bridge to the village shop.

She could feel the sun caressing her skin as she walked home along the river. There was a heron standing on the banks peering greedily into the trout stream, and she noticed that the jumps across at the riding school had received a fresh coat of paint. It would be fun to watch

by
Kate
Clayton

I

the jumping, she thought. There was always something to do in a village.

She managed not to think about Richard until evening, when the thatchers had gone and she had the cottage to herself.

Then the usual bleak desolation washed over her.

She remembered his lop-sided smile and the way he could be tender and funny and kind all at the same time, and the tears welled up in her eyes and rolled down her cheeks, so that she had to put down the basin in which she was whipping eggs for her supper, and fumble for a tissue.

She blew her nose hard and switched on the cooker determindly.

Then she heard a little pattering noise behind her, and discovered she had a visitor. He was a Beagle; a brown and white patchy Beagle, with bright, mischievous yellow eyes, long floppy ears and a waving tail. From his mouth dangled a long string of sausages!

"Oh, you wicked fellow." She choked, laughter breaking through her tears. "What have you been up to, and where have you come from?"

She made a sudden movement, and the dog, obviously well aware of his wickedness, moved sharply aside, dropping the sausages as he went.

"Hi, come back!" she called, but it was useless. The miscreant had vanished through one of the many gaps in the hedge.

She picked up the sausages and gave them a careful scrutiny. Only one was irretrievably mangled. The rest appeared to be unviolated.

She rinsed them under the tap, dried them on a piece of kitchen roll, and put them into the fridge. Who knew if some irate villager might next appear demanding his stolen property!

But no-one disturbed her solitude, and she went to bed early only to sleep fitfully despite the comfort of Aunt Rhona's bed.

PHILIPPA was awakened in the morning by the twittering of the house martins in the thatch; not to mention the sound of farm machinery, milk lorries and cockerels!

She lay listening for a while. Then she rose and dressed and went out into the garden.

There was dew on the uncut grass in the orchard, and the rings of daffodils which Uncle Patrick had lovingly planted round the apple trees made patches of brightness.

The morning air was so fresh and clean she stood for a while inhaling great quantities of it, allowing her breath to escape slowly, and feeling unexpectedly exhilarated.

She realised she was hungry then, and went back indoors to make coffee and toast. She was just settling down to eat when a head appeared at the open window.

It was an exceedingly untidy head, and seemed to be streaked with paint. Underneath it was a lean brown face, two alert hazel eyes, a mouth which curved humorously, and a dark unshaven chin.

She realised in a flash this must be Fred's nephew, and hoped his work would present a tidier appearance than his person.

She went over to the window.

"Good morning," she said. "Would you mind coming round to the back door?"

"My name's Roger Lawson," he began as he stood on the step.

"Mine's Philippa Barlow. Mrs Houseman is my aunt, and I'm looking after the cottage for her."

"I see," he said.

"Would you like to look at the bathroom?"

"Not particularly," he replied, with a quirk of his dark brows. "Unless you really want me to."

She stared at him, resenting the amusement in his eyes.

"I suppose you *are* the painter?" she said acidly.

His grin deepened.

"I'm *a* painter," he said, "but somehow, I don't think I'm *the* painter. In other words, I'm not a walls-and-windows man."

She felt herself go pink.

"You mean . . ." she stammered. "You mean . . . you're not Fred's nephew?"

"Not to my knowledge," he said facetiously.

"I wish you'd stop trying to be funny," she said, "and tell me why you're here."

His grin faded, and he stood to mock attention.

I'M sorry," he apologised. "But if I can't see the funny side of it I'll go up the wall. I've been up since the crack of dawn searching for my dog. He's a brown and white Beagle pup, and he suffers from wanderlust, amongst other defects. I don't suppose you've seen anything of him?"

"Actually," she said, her mouth twitching, "a dog of this description did . . . er . . . drop in last night. He only stayed about half a minute, and he . . . er, left these." She reached into the fridge and extracted the sausages. "I presume they belong to you?"

He groaned.

"If only they did," he said. "Life at this moment would be considerably less complicated, and the finding of Havoc would be less urgent."

"Havoc?" she echoed.

"Havoc is the name of my dog. Very appropriate, as you may possibly have realised."

"Our meeting was very brief," she said demurely. "He seemed in a hurry."

"He usually is," Havoc's master said, "mainly of necessity. If you'll excuse me, I think I should be on my way while the trail's hot. I shudder to think what he may be up to this very minute."

"Have you time for a cup of coffee?" she said, repenting of her former churlishness.

"A cup of coffee could strengthen my armour," he agreed.

Their tête-a-tête was interrupted by the arrival of the thatchers.

"Adios . . ." Roger said as he left. "Many thanks for the coffee. If you don't mind wrapping it up a bit, I'll take the evidence with me. I don't see why you should be incriminated."

She wrapped the sausages in a piece of foil and handed them to him.

"Good hunting," she called as he went out of the door.

WHEN she'd tidied up and dispensed coffee to the two on the roof, Philippa decided to drive into Dorchester. The lanes were lined with wild white parsley which, in turn, was intermingled with bright pink campions.

She slowed down as she passed the famous Martyr's Tree, where the first trade unionists had staged their ill-fated protest, and swung out on to the main road.

The towers of the ancient market town loomed against an azure sky, and she had to circle round and round its narrow streets with their Roman remains before she could find anywhere to park.

She deliberately didn't hurry, and found a little old-world café for lunch. On the journey home she took a different route, passing through several tiny thatched villages with their clustering cottages and well-kept greens, and wondered how much they had changed since the time of Hardy.

When she got home the thatchers had finished for the day. Discarded reed lay in untidy piles over the front garden awaiting collection, and she saw that the whole of the back roof was now completed.

In the porch Philippa found a note, thanking her for her hospitality of the morning and inviting her to a sausage supper at seven o'clock that same evening. The address was No. 3 Caravan, Church Field, and it was signed "Havoc."

Philippa hesitated with the note in her hand for a full half minute, hating the idea of being alone all evening. But in the end she screwed it up and flung it in the bin. She wasn't having any more entanglements at the moment. It was simply asking for trouble.

Shortly afterwards the doorbell rang. Philippa hurried through the hall, but the figure she caught sight of through the frosted glass panel of the front door made the blood drain away from her face.

She saw straightaway, with a gasp of relief, that it had been just a chance likeness. The blond hair, the beard . . .

"I say . . . are you all right?" the newcomer asked.

"Yes, I'm quite all right. For a moment I thought you were somebody else. Someone I knew a while ago . . . I think you must be Rod?"

"That's right," he said. "I've come to make a start on the bathroom, if that's all right with you."

Philippa's legs were still trembling as she and Rod discussed the work which had to be done.

"Are you sure you're all right?" he asked her again. "Could I get you something . . . a cup of tea perhaps?"

"No . . . I . . . I think I'll go out for a little while if you can carry on. I've got rather a headache, and the fresh air . . ."

"You do that," he said. "I'll stay until ten o'clock. There's a fair bit of filling-in to do."

PHILIPPA didn't realise she'd walked past the churchyard and into the campers' field, until Havoc raced up to her with an ecstatic welcome.

"I'm glad you came," a voice said. It was Roger Lawson.

He was lounging on the steps of his van, a blue sweater thrown across his shoulders. He looked so different, she hardly recognised him. His hair was smooth and entirely paintless, and his blue velvet cords were as immaculate as his blue silk shirt. He wasn't a handsome man, but he looked elegant and distinguished.

"Come in," he said, "and have a drink."

Inside, the van was elegant too. She wondered how on earth he achieved it. There was good china and exquisite glassware on the little drop-down table in the window.

"You were pretty sure of me," she remarked, noticing the two place settings. "I didn't intend to come."

He placed a cushion behind her back, and handed her a sherry.

"I'm an eternal optimist." He grinned. "Artists have to be."

Later he produced steaks and a delicious salad.

"What about the sausages?" she enquired. The drink had restored her confidence, and she was ready to play along with his mood.

"I buried them," he said in a sepulchral whisper.

She giggled.

"I wonder whose they were."

"I dread to think. Promise never to split?"

They laughed companionably, and Philippa found herself able to relax.

When he showed her his paintings she was filled with delight and surprise.

November

LONG are your days, November,
 cold and grey;
Your mists of gloomy dimness shroud the
 day,
And constant are your rains, from morn
 to night.
Yet when the evening lamps are lit, how
 bright
 The pavements light and shine,
 November.

Wild are you ways, November; storm
 and fret
Your howling gales and wailing winds
 — and yet
Not all the fragrant freshness of the
 spring,
Not all the sun-drenched hours of
 summer bring
 Your hearthside cosiness, like you,
 November.

Frances Carr.

They were so different from what she'd expected. He illustrated children's books, he explained, and had tried to produce a style that was original.

"You've succeeded too," she said. "I've never seen anything quite like them. They're sort of . . . ethereal, shadowy . . . exactly right for children, because the colour is there just the same."

"You've made my day," he said. "I had a tough time persuading my agent to see it the way you've done."

Philippa found herself sorry when ten o'clock came, and she had to go.

"Thank you," she said. "I've really enjoyed myself."

"I'll walk you home through the wood," he said. "Havoc can have his twilight bark. He can't indulge on the site, it upsets the neighbours. You know what Beagles are."

Because she hadn't brought a jacket, he draped his blue sweater across her shoulders, tying the long woollen arms across her chest.

"Mustn't get cold," he said in a gentle, teasing voice, and she knew if she'd had any sense she should cut and run before it was too late.

Fred's nephew had made great strides in the bathroom, but she was glad he didn't stay to chat. The uncanny likeness still disturbed her, and she felt uneasy in his company.

THE following afternoon, Roger Lawson strolled down and asked her if she'd have any objection to him sketching the cottage. It was just what he needed for his Gingerbread House illustrations.

"Of course," she said. "You can tie Havoc to the front fence."

It gave her a lovely warm feeling to see him sitting on his stool, sketchbook on his knee. There was certainly no time to brood with the thatchers on the roof, Rod in the bathroom and Roger in the lane. The day seemed a positive whirl of coffee, tea and chat.

When the Gingerbread House was finished, he asked her if she would like to come with him to the Cove, inspiration seeking.

"You find all sorts of interesting things on the beach. Shells, starfish, pebbles, bits of driftwood . . . even seaweed."

They didn't find any particular treasures, but it was great fun scrambling amongst the rocks, the wind blowing her hair, and his hand, cool and firm, when the going was rough.

They called in at the Crab and Lobster on the way home and had a bar snack. There was a notice over the fireplace advertising a Smugglers Ball the following Saturday.

"I think we should come to that," he said. "I have to go to London tomorrow for a few days to see my agent, but I'll be back by lunchtime on Saturday."

"What fun," Philippa said, and her eyes sparkled in a way they hadn't done for a long time. "But what about Havoc? Would you like me to take care of him while you're away?"

He rolled his eyes heavenwards.

"You don't know what you'd be taking on. I think he must have been an escapologist in a previous incarnation; but thanks for the offer. Actually I've bribed the boys at No. 2 van to take him for walks and feed him. The rest of the time, he's going to be shut up."

While Roger was in London, she decided to have another trip to Dorchester. She had library books to return, and she'd decided to buy a new dress for the Smugglers Ball.

There was a little shop, Town & Country Boutique, in the High Street which sold the clothes she liked.

The dress she chose was patterned with seashells and starfishes, and was exactly what she'd had in mind. It would remind her of the day at the cove which she knew she would always think of with affection because it had played such a big part in the healing of her heart.

When she got back, there was a note from Rod to ring her aunt. The news was bad. Uncle Patrick had died the previous night. It was not unexpected, but a shock just the same. The funeral would be on Saturday.

"I'll come first thing in the morning," she said. "I know what a lot there will be to do."

As she packed, her heart was heavy for Aunt Rhona; and for herself, for Uncle Patrick had been a great favourite. She set about clearing her own belongings, popping them into the open hatchback of the car, which was parked close to the back door.

There was a piece of steak left in the fridge which she didn't feel like cooking. What a pity Havoc wasn't around. Absently she wrapped it up and stowed it between her cases.

Thinking about Havoc made her realise she couldn't let Roger know she'd been called away. Neither the thatchers nor Rod would be working on Saturday, the cottage would be dark and unoccupied when he called in the evening.

Whatever could she do? If only she had his London address or phone number, but it had never occurred to her to ask for it.

THE next morning the weather had broken. A storm was starting. She could see lightning, blue and forked over the long wood, and hoped the caravans would be all right with so many trees around.

She sighed as she got into the car, switching on the lights and the windscreen wipers. She'd have to step on it if she was to reach her aunt's house before dark.

The rain poured until she reached the New Forest, when it eased off very slightly. She pulled into the first garage she saw for petrol, and it was then that she realised she was carrying a passenger. It was the little snuffling sound from the direction of the hatchback which gave her the clue!

"Havoc!" she gasped, as the tips of two patchy paws gripped the back seat, followed by one and a half cocked ears and one yellow eye. "How on earth did you get into the car?"

She watched helplessly as the rest of the Beagle emerged inch by inch, until he was sitting beside her in the passenger seat quivering with shame. Round his mouth were the remains of the paper in which she had wrapped the steak.

He rolled his eyes upwards mournfully and gave himself a little shake. As he did so, the metal disc attached to his collar chinked! To Philippa it was the sweetest sound on earth.

"Oh Havoc!" she said, scribbling down the telephone number which was inscribed beneath the London address, "you'll never know what you've just done for me."

The garage man, watching the slowly-forming queue of umbrellas outside the telephone kiosk alongside the pumps, wondered how on earth two people could find so much to say to each other. But when he saw the radiance on the girl's face as she emerged, he began to understand! □

DECISION of the HEART

by Christine Maxwell

ANYONE seeing the small village of Tillydrem for the first time
might well imagine it to be a backwater, the sort of place where
life flows by in an uneventful fashion, and where little of note
happens from one year's end to another.

Anyone getting to know the place properly will soon discover it isn't
like that at all!

For one thing, Tillydrem folk are always ready to try something new.
Sometimes that proves a mistake. I remember, for instance, the
bulb-growing competition at the Women's Guild which resulted in
several members not speaking to each other for weeks afterwards! That
was one event not tried again.

On the other hand, when the Guild started having a winter outing to a

theatre in Edinburgh, that was such a success it has taken place every year since — even if the good ladies did get stuck in a snowdrift on the way home one time!

As for the new event tried by the local Dog Show Committee this spring, no one can say if it will ever be repeated. When it was first suggested at a meeting, the reaction of some members wasn't at all favourable, and some still think the whole thing was a mistake.

For whoever heard of a cat and dog show being held at the same time in the same building? Cats and dogs together? The idea was absurd!

"It would be fair pandemonium!" Ronald Kerr exclaimed. He was the farmer from Croftside, who was presiding at the meeting.

"The dogs would be barking to get at the cats, and the cats would be yowling and scrabbling to get away from the dogs," he declared.

Oh no, much better to keep this small spring show confined to dogs, mostly working ones at that, since sheep-dogs and gun-dogs accounted for the bulk of the entries.

But cats! The competitors weren't likely to be the rangy farm animals which did useful work among the mice and rats. They would be pet pussies that did nothing at all for a living, just sat about looking decorative.

So thought most of the farmers present. But they hadn't a chance against the two ladies at the meeting. It was the older one, Miss Atkinson, who had made the suggestion, and now waited patiently until the protests died down.

"May I continue?" she asked then. "Thank you. As you all know, I'm a dog person myself. But I feel it isn't fair that there's nothing at all here for cat lovers.

"I'm not suggesting that the animals are in the same room. The dogs can be in the large hall as usual, and the cats in this room. With the kitchen and the vestibule in between the two rooms, I'm sure one lot will hardly hear the other."

"I think it's a great idea," Moira Kerr supported her eagerly.

MOIRA was twenty and acted as secretary to the committee. It was well known that she could coax anything out of her indulgent father and she set to work on him now.

"Come on, Dad," she wheedled. "Let's try it once. I'll put Ginger into the show and I'm almost certain he'll bring a prize back to Croftside. You'll be pleased then."

"I'm quite willing to take charge of all the arrangements," Miss Atkinson stated. "I'll also take responsibility if it's a failure."

"And what can you do against two determined women?" Ronald Kerr lamented later to his wife, as he sat at home with her and his daughter over their late cup of tea.

Mrs Kerr was plump and placid, and she thought the cat show quite a good idea.

"Anyway, Ginger thinks it's a good idea." Moira laughed, as she bent to stroke the large, orange-coloured cat lying stretched out in front of the fire.

Presently Mr and Mrs Kerr went off to bed, leaving Moira busily writing the minutes of the meeting before she forgot what had been said. It was always as well to do this at once, and she hadn't much time during the day.

But Moira enjoyed her job as secretary at the big, new hospital five miles away along the Dremlachie road, and she liked coming home each night to the farmhouse.

A LL the same, there was a problem in her life at present. When she had finished the minutes, she sat for a while doing nothing at all, her pretty face clouding a little as she stared absently down at the words she had written.

It was so difficult to know what to do, yet the decision she had to make was a hundred times more important than whether or not to hold a cat show.

What should she say to Nigel Spence next time she saw him? If only she knew! She'd been going out with Nigel now for some time, and all the other girls thought her lucky.

Tall, handsome, with a good job — Nigel in every way seemed likely to make a good husband. It was nearly a year now since he had first come to Croftside and advised her father about the purchase of a new potato lifter.

"That chap knows his job," Ronald Kerr had said approvingly, after the lifter had proved a success. "There's not a question you ask about farm machinery that he can't answer."

It was a week ago, at the Young Farmers' Dance, that Nigel had asked her to marry him. She had been vaguely expecting the proposal, yet when it came she felt worried.

"I . . . I don't know, Nigel," she had got out awkwardly in reply. "I'd like to wait a bit . . . I mean to think about it for a while."

Nigel had pulled her into his arms and kissed her tenderly, agreeing that he would wait for his answer for a week or two.

"Don't make it too long, darling," he had pleaded. "And you'll say yes, won't you?"

"I'll think about it," she had repeated cautiously.

Now as she sat alone in the quiet room, she wondered again why she hesitated. Weren't some of the happiest marriages those where there was a little uncertainty at first? Look at her parents, for example.

"Your father asked me six times before I agreed," Mrs Kerr had said often. "I still couldn't make up my mind if I liked him enough. It was after my mother died and I felt lonely that I said yes at last. It was the best thing I've ever done," she would add softly.

Thinking it over now, Moira decided she must be like her mother. She would say yes in the end to Nigel and they would be happy together.

"But I'll wait till after this show is safely over," she resolved. "Time enough then to think about weddings!"

Late as it was, she now had to write a letter to the new assistant vet at Dremlachie, asking if he would be so kind as to come and judge the cat classes for them.

"He seems a suitable person," Miss Atkinson had said at the meeting. "And since his boss is judging the dogs they can come over from Dremlachie together."

As Moira began writing the letter, she found herself smiling over what Miss Atkinson had told her later about the new vet.

"His name's James Henderson," Miss Atkinson had informed her. "Rather like the name of the vet on that TV series, isn't it? Poor man, he told me when he worked in Glasgow people used to tease him by calling him Mr Herriot, and one silly woman even pretended her dog was calling him Uncle Henderson, like the one in the series."

Though Moira smiled, she felt rather sorry for the young man, and hoped no one here would tease him over what was really a very shadowy resemblance to the TV character.

I T was a few days before she received a reply from James Henderson, and then it was a phone call one evening.

"Is that Miss Moira Kerr?" an unknown voice asked. "It's James Henderson. Thank you for your letter, Miss Kerr, and I'll be very pleased to be judge at your show."

He paused momentarily before going on.

"The only thing is I've never done this sort of thing before. Can you tell me exactly what to look for in judging a cat?"

"I'm not too sure either," Moira confessed. "It's a new venture for Tillydrem. I should think just general appearance, and good health, which you'll know all about, of course. No obvious defects. It's just a very informal sort of affair," she added.

"Oh, well, that's fine," he returned.

"There are only the three classes," she went on, "long-haired, short-haired and children's pets. Then Miss Atkinson, who is organising the show, is awarding an extra prize for the best of these three winners."

"I see. Thanks a lot, Miss Kerr, and I'll look forward to meeting you that Saturday."

They chatted on for a few minutes and when the brief conversation was over, Moira decided James Henderson seemed a good choice to be judge at the informal little show. She wondered what he looked like. He had a pleasant voice anyway . . .

Soon the entries began to come in. Eventually there were 22 altogether for the cat classes. Moira was quite pleased to notice only five were for the long-haired cats. That gave Ginger a good chance of winning a prize!

Industriously, she brushed and combed his thick coat every day, and discouraged his prowls through dusty parts of the farm buildings.

"Remember you're a show cat now," she told him firmly.

All but one entry came from local people. But there was one from further away and Moira studied it doubtfully. Who was this unknown Miss Martindale, entering a cat called "Esmeralda of Edelton?" The homely Tillydrem show wasn't intended for cats with grand names who probably went to big important shows all over the country.

"That's just what this one is," Miss Atkinson groaned when Moira showed her the entry. "I've heard of Miss Martindale. She breeds cats and exhibits them at the very top shows. What's she bothering about our one for, I'd like to know?"

"Anyway, her cat is short haired, so it won't be competing against Ginger," Moira consoled herself.

All the same, as the time of the show drew near, she found herself wishing this particular entry hadn't come in. A complete stranger, seeing the way things went on in Tillydrem for the first time, might well not approve.

Why?

WHEN feeling at my very best,
　　When the house is clean and
　　neat,
When I've lots and lots of leisure,
　　And I'm not run off my feet,
No-one comes to see me —
　　I have put it to the test —
But when I'm extra busy,
　　When I'm worried and oppressed,
When my fruit-cake in the oven
　　Decides to droop and sag,
When I have no time to dress with care,
　　And feel an awful hag —
When my stocking springs a ladder,
　　From the ankle to the knee —
Why is it that my friends decide
　　To come and call on me?
　　　　　　　　　— Miriam Eker.

THERE was another worry for Moira.

Nigel Spence appeared with an invitation to go across to Dundee with him on the evening of the show, to see a new play that was being staged there.

"Oh, not that night," Moira protested. "It would be such a rush to get ready, Nigel. I have to help to put things straight again in the hall when both shows are over, and people usually linger on at these affairs. I thought you knew that was the day of the show."

"I did know," Nigel told her. "I doubt if your cat show will last long anyway. Moira, you must come. I've got the tickets, and you did say you'd like to see that show."

"I know. If only it had been some other night!" She sighed.

"Well, I'll come along some time in the afternoon and see how you're getting on," Nigel warned. "And it's time now you gave me your answer to what I asked you before."

Oh, dear, Moira thought. Perhaps it was time, but she didn't know what to answer . . .

At last it was Saturday afternoon. Looking round the smaller hall, Moira felt satisfied by the neat arrangement of boxes in which the cats were contained.

Amid all the home-made boxes there was one very professional-looking one, with a large, sleek, black cat inside. Esmeralda of Edelton, no doubt! A middle-aged woman with a glum expression stood guarding the box.

From her face it was obvious that Miss Martindale didn't think much of this set-up! Moira's heart sank. They should really have sought advice on the running of a cat show. Perhaps things were done differently from when it was dogs . . .

"Moira," Ronald Kerr's voice came from behind her, "here's Mr Henderson looking for you. He got in amongst the dogs by mistake!"

THE young man who came forward gave Moira a friendly smile. He had rather a nice face, she thought, even if he wasn't as good looking as Nigel.

"Hello, Miss Kerr," he began. "I see everything's ready."

"Yes, it shouldn't take you too long." Moira smiled back.

But somehow they started to chat, and a few minutes went past. James Henderson was enjoying his work in this district. It was a change from town work, and he'd always wanted more to do with the larger animals, like cattle and horses.

They looked at each other, finding a mutual liking. But the moment was broken abruptly when Nigel Spence shouldered his way through the crowd of people now gathered in this room to look at the cats.

"Got your judging over, darling?" he asked Moira. "Has your pet got a prize?"

"We — we haven't begun yet," Moira got out awkwardly, wishing Nigel hadn't mentioned Ginger.

She hadn't intended James Henderson to know she was competing until after the judging. And somehow she didn't like Nigel calling her "darling" in that possessive fashion. She didn't belong to him yet! Turning away, she spoke formally to the young vet.

"Will you begin now, Mr Henderson?"

"Yes, certainly. Please come round with me," the young man said firmly. "I may need your assistance."

"Yes, of course," Moira said hastily. "I'll see you later, Nigel."

"You'd better!" Nigel said. "This is all a ridiculous waste of time!"

Moira looked after him uneasily as he strode out of the hall. Why was he angry? Hadn't she explained about the show, and warned him she might not be able to go out with him that evening? New doubts came into her mind. She certainly wasn't going to marry a man who must get his own way all the time.

Now, however, she must take James Henderson to inspect the long-haired cats. Fortunately Ginger proved to be far and away the best looking in the small class, and the red ticket was laid on top of his box. The blue ticket, for second prize, was awarded to the stolid animal usually to be seen in the grocer's shop.

That would please Mr Jameson, Moira thought, for he'd been telling his customers he didn't really think Podger was classy enough for a win!

There was no doubt either as to the winner in the short-haired class. Esmeralda of Edelton was streets ahead of the rest. Finally, there was the class for children's pets to be judged.

THERE was a good entry here, mostly of kittens, and one young owner had taken his pet out of the box and was now cradling it in his arms.

"Put Pip back in his box for a few minutes, Mike," Moira said gently.

The boy did so. He was a small, pale nine-year-old, and there was a desperate longing in his eyes as he gazed anxiously up at the vet. Moira longed to tell James Henderson about the tragedy in Mike's life, and how winning a prize would mean something very special to him. But no, it would never do for a prize to be given away out of sympathy.

She needn't have worried. Gravely, James handed the red ticket to Mike. A sudden radiance spread over the pale little face. Taking the kitten out of the box again, Mike dashed across the room to where an elderly couple stood watching.

"Granny! Grandpa!" he cried. "Pip's won first prize!"

The spectators laughed, but a round of applause showed this was a popular win. James looked inquiringly at Moira.

"Mike hasn't been long in Tillydrem," she told him quietly. "He came to live with his grandparents when his parents were killed in a car crash away down in England. They were on their way home from buying a kitten for his birthday and in some miraculous way neither Mike nor the kitten was really hurt."

She sighed.

"Pip has helped Mike to get over the shock of it all, just by being something that came with him from his former life, something alive of his very own. I'm so glad you gave him the prize."

"I'm glad, too," James said. "Poor little chap —"

He was interrupted by Miss Martindale who confronted him now.

"Isn't there a prize for Best in Show?" she demanded. "Isn't it going to be awarded?"

But she would have been wiser to keep a watchful eye on her property, for four-year-old Sandy Gillon was wandering along the row of boxes, wishing he could get one of these nice pussies out to play with him.

The first thing he'd done after he'd left his parents in the other room and come in here was to unlock and open the lid of the piano. It was easy! Now his eye fell on the catch securing the box where the lovely, black pussy sat. His clever little fingers got to work and the front of the box swung open in no time at all.

EVEN Sandy was startled by what happened next. Esmeralda shot from the box like a rocket, streaking across the room so fast that somebody screamed. Panic stricken, Esmeralda leapt up on to the piano. A wild discord of notes frightened her still more, and she sprang for the long curtains which the Guild provided for cold winter evenings.

With the agility of a circus acrobat, she climbed them nimbly, settling herself on a ledge above the curtain pole, hissing and spitting.

Poor Miss Martindale! No wonder she was cross! It took a step-ladder, ascended by herself, before Esmeralda could be retrieved and returned to her box.

Not even the award of Best in Show mollified her, as she exchanged heated words with Miss Atkinson about the proper way a cat show should be conducted.

And now Nigel was back in the room and hurrying towards her.

"Come on, Moira, let's get out of this shambles," he urged. "I knew the thing would be a flop."

"Nigel, that isn't true!" Moira gasped.

No, for hadn't everyone had a wonderful laugh at the cat climbing the curtains? Hadn't Pip winning a prize been the first thing to bring a smile to Mike's face since he came to Tillydrem? It hadn't been a flop at all, just one more Tillydrem event where something unexpected happened.

And something even more important . . . this afternoon had shown Moira that in spite of his undoubted charm, Nigel wasn't the man to make her happy in marriage. Her doubts had been justified. But how on earth was she going to tell him, right in the midst of a crowd of people?

"Once and for all, are you coming?" he muttered as she hesitated.

"Not just now," she whispered back.

"It's obvious Tillydrem's affairs mean more to you than I do!" he accused her.

"Perhaps they do," she murmured unhappily.

There was no need to say more. Nigel marched out of the hall and Moira discovered that she was trembling. Scenes like this were upsetting, and it was an effort to pull herself together when she saw James Henderson coming towards her.

"I'll have to go now, Miss Kerr," he said. "I looked into the other room for a minute and my boss has finished judging the dogs. He wants to get off back to Dremlachie. But I'll be seeing you again soon, I hope?"

It might have been the scene with Nigel, or the surprising little throb of pleasure Moira got as she looked back into a pair of steady grey eyes . . . or anything! Whatever it was, she now addressed the young man in a way she'd never intended.

"Oh, yes, I hope so, Mr Herriot," she answered him. "And thank you very much for helping us today."

James Henderson smiled. He realised she didn't know what she had called him, and the strange thing was that this time he didn't mind in the least. He felt pretty sure she wouldn't be calling him Mr anything for long! □

143

Echoes From The Past

by Gillian Fraser

L OUISE RAEBURN had bought herself a retiral gift. She admitted
that a modern dining room suite was an expensive indulgence, but
with more time on her hands, she wanted something fresh in the
house to go with the changes in her life.

In her delight at finding the suite she wanted, Louise had taken the
risk of being able to match it with her older furniture. After some
judicious switching around, she'd succeeded, except for one thing — her
antique roll-top desk. It didn't seem to fit in, yet she couldn't move it
because of its bulk.

Louise wondered if she should sell it, but didn't have the heart, for it
was a real family heirloom which had spanned the years between past
and present.

Time had flown too fast for Louise and now she was at one of life's
many crossroads, uncertain of which way to turn. And with so many
spare hours on her hands, memories were returning which should have
been long forgotten. What might have been was uppermost in her mind

when she thought of Hal and his dashing ways. Louise had been the envy of her friends when Hal and she had started courting seriously.

Even the desk was a reminder of these days when she'd tucked away his love letters in one of its secret drawers. Not any more, though; she'd destroyed them years ago.

Pamela was horrified at the suggestion of selling the desk.

"It would be like losing a member of your family. I've always loved that old desk. When I was young I even thought there was magic in it." She laughed.

"I always wondered where the lid went when it rolled up." Louise agreed.

"You're right, Pam, the old desk is rather precious. All I needed was someone as sensible as you to remind me. Now, if you'll close the lid on all my dark secrets, we can have some tea."

Pamela tugged unsuccessfully.

"I'm sorry, Aunt Louise." She gasped. "It seems to be jammed."

"Well, just leave it, dear. Maybe the wood's warped — I wouldn't worry."

But Pamela was conscious of her aunt's anxious glances towards the desk during tea and was determined to do something about it.

T HIS was the time of day Louise loved best, when Pamela was home and they were together in close companionship. Pamela had been under her wing ever since her parents were tragically killed and they were able to draw comfort from each other.

But their world, although a warm, private one, was fragile, with reality lurking just round the corner. Louise Raeburn understood only too well that it couldn't last for ever.

Eventually, Pam would marry and leave to start her own life. There was no sign of that yet, though, as Pamela was enjoying her job in the flower shop with little time for young men in her life. Despite this, a question kept nagging at Louise.

How shall I react when someone comes to snatch Pam away from me, she wondered.

Pam's main concern at the moment was repairing the desk. Next morning in the shop, she was anxiously running her finger through the Yellow Pages. The other assistant, Beryl, quizzed her. "Needing some work done, Pam?"

"The lid's jammed on Aunt Louise's roll-top desk. I don't suppose you could recommend anyone, could you?"

"My dad always goes to Lindsay's," Beryl told her.

"Where are they?"

"In Ross Street." Beryl's eyes took on an added sparkle. "If you go to Lindsay's, ask for Scott. He's fantastic."

Pamela chuckled.

"As a cabinet maker or a human being?"

"Both," Beryl replied innocently. "Dad thinks he's a good craftsman and I like his looks."

Pamela, her interest aroused, decided to give Lindsay's a try. She

K   145

found the shop tucked away unobtrusively and the inside, once her eyes had become used to the gloom, was a shambles. Off-cuts of wood lay everywhere, and the atmosphere was thick with sawdust.

Pam thought of the desk, and was beginning to have second thoughts. Somehow she couldn't equate this mess with efficient working.

Her confidence was lessened further as she waited impatiently for someone to attend to her. As the minutes ticked by, her anger mounted, but instead of walking out she stormed through to the workshop, despite the no entry sign.

The loud warning shout was too late to prevent her tripping over a plank. Pam stumbled only to find herself supported by two strong arms. Concerned eyes looked into hers.

"That was a silly thing to do. You could have hurt yourself. Didn't you see the sign?"

"The only way to get any service around here was to ignore it!" Pamela retorted.

The young man's face relaxed into a smile.

"Sorry, I'm up to my eyes in work at the moment — I didn't hear a thing. What can I do for you?"

As Pamela explained, the young man scratched his head thoughtfully, sawdust cascading from his dark hair.

"Repairing antiques isn't really our line of work. We deal mostly with shop fitting."

PAMELA was about to turn away when she noticed him grinning at her — it was infuriating, almost mocking. She felt herself colouring under his gaze and made up her mind that, if he was Scott Lindsay, she'd rather have nothing more to do with him.

"You're not going yet, are you?" he asked in some surprise. "I mean, you come into my life, fall into my arms. You surely can't just walk out again?"

Pamela bridled at his words.

"I can and I will — just watch me!"

"Would you stay if I offered to repair your desk?" he asked contritely.

"But you said . . ."

"I know, but I never said I wouldn't do it. I have to be cautious, that's all. My grandfather runs things, so any decision would have to be his. I'm just the hired help, overworked and underpaid. Scott Lindsay's the name."

"I thought it would be," Pamela said acidly.

"That sounds ominous!" Scott chuckled. "Has my reputation gone before me?"

"From a mutual friend."

"Aren't you going to tell me your name?" he asked. "I need to get in touch with you about the desk." Again that infuriating grin.

"Pamela Raeburn. You'll find me in the flower shop on the High Street."

Scott watched her go.

I must be losing my grip, he thought, that line of chat usually works. But he put thoughts of Pamela to the back of his mind, for he had another pressing problem — grandfather.

S COTT LINDSAY couldn't understand his grandfather's attitude. Since Scott had finished his apprenticeship, the older man seemed to have become resentful, yet they'd always got on splendidly before. Since his grandmother died, Scott had moved in with him, and now this was beginning to mar their relationship.

Hal Lindsay was annoyed.

"You know how much work we have on hand — I'd rather you didn't take on wee jobs like that. Any joiner could cope with it."

"But she didn't come to just any joiner, Grandad. She came to us. We were highly recommended by her friend."

Hal arched one eyebrow.

"She, did you say?"

"Yes."

"Attractive, I suppose?"

"Not so sure, a bit too reserved for me," Scott replied.

Hal sighed.

"There's a lot of me in you, lad! I could never resist a bonnie face either. Take my advice and leave well alone or you'll just be storing up grief for yourself." Then he looked at Scott and shrugged.

"Bring the desk in," he capitulated. "No harm in having a look at it."

Hal Lindsay smiled inwardly. Louise Raeburn had had a lovely old roll-top desk, but it surely couldn't be that one. For a moment he was tempted to ask Scott then thought better of it. The less he reminisced on Louise Raeburn, the better for his peace of mind.

Hal stalked off leaving a very puzzled Scott. His Grandad Lindsay was never one to pass on advice, yet suddenly words of warning were pouring from him, and on Scott's favourite subject, too — girls. I wonder why, Scott thought.

*　　*　　*　　*

"How very thoughtful of you," Louise Raeburn told Pam. "Arranging to have the desk repaired."

"I just wish I hadn't gone to that place!" Pamela exploded. "That Scott Lindsay's arrogant, conceited, impudent . . ."

"Which means you're quite taken with him," Louise interrupted.

"Of course it doesn't," Pamela cried. "He's detestable." Then her face relaxed into a smile. "Well, I suppose he is quite good looking under all that dirt and sawdust."

"You did say Lindsay?"

"Yes, the place in Ross Street."

Louise felt a sudden coldness. How many years had flown by since her connections with the Lindsay family? She felt herself panicking.

"Won't a joiner be expensive, dear? Couldn't we fix it ourselves?"

"No," Pamela said firmly. "That desk means a lot to you. It must be mended properly." She smiled. "Didn't you tell me that's where you hid all your love letters? Just who was this secret passion you've been hiding from me all these years?"

Unwittingly, Pam had opened the floodgates of the past. The memories stung, accentuated by the void retiring had brought to her life.

Pam looked at her questioningly. Yes, Louise thought, she has every right to know, if she and Scott Lindsay want to be friends. Anyway, there would be relief in telling someone as sympathetic as Pamela.

"Hal Lindsay and I grew up together, our families were neighbours. He and I were in each other's pockets from childhood onwards, same class at school, similar interests."

A fleeting smile crossed Louise Raeburn's features.

"I think both sets of parents saw the end of this to be our marriage. You know the sort of thing, childhood romance spilling over into adulthood. I think Hal and I believed it too, because we'd actually talked about becoming engaged. That's when Emily Brand arrived on the scene." Louise sighed.

"You mean he dropped you for someone else after promising to marry you?" Pamela gasped.

"Oh no, dear, we weren't engaged," Louise corrected, trying to play the situation down.

"How could anyone be so cruel?" Pam protested.

"In hindsight," Louise Raeburn explained, "it was the best thing that could have happened. I don't think Hal and I were really suited. I was quiet, reserved, rather like you, while Hal was harum scarum.

"Still, from what I heard over the years," Louise went on, "he and Emily were happy enough. Hal's on his own now — Emily died last year."

Pam suggested she could still cancel the order, but Louise wouldn't hear of it.

"I'm grateful for your concern," she told Pam. "But I don't suppose Hal Lindsay would even remember about us now."

PAM RAEBURN was busy in the flower shop making up some bridal bouquets when her friend Beryl whispered something to her excitedly. "He's here, asking for you!"

"Who is?"

Beryl pointed discreetly towards Scott Lindsay, who was hovering near the counter.

"How did you manage to hook him, Pam? Oh, he's so dreamy."

Scott was smiling broadly.

"I've confirmed the order with Grandfather, now if you'll give me your address, I'll arrange to have the desk picked up."

Pam supplied it in a cool manner, which Scott hardly seemed to notice. Instead he looked round then paid her an outrageous compliment.

"You're like a flower amongst flowers, Pamela Raeburn."

She felt herself blushing furiously under his mocking gaze, determined that as soon as the desk was repaired, Scott Lindsay would be out of her life for ever.

Yet she felt he was challenging her in some way to respond, and she was interested enough in him to want to react to this. When the desk was repaired, it would be too late.

She wanted to answer him there and then, but the shop was filling up with customers. When she looked up again, he'd gone and Pam was conscious of a feeling of loss.

★　★　★　★

That evening, Hal Lindsay and his grandson were sitting over supper browsing over the day's events. Scott told him about the desk.

"You don't look very pleased about it. I thought that's what you wanted, to impress some bonnie lassie?"

Hal frowned.

"I'm not making any impression on the bonnie lassie, that's the trouble," Scott replied moodily. "Maybe you're right, Grandad, too much grief. I think I'll stay single." He shook his head sadly. "I like Pamela Raeburn, but for some reason she doesn't seem to care for me at all."

Hal arched an eyebrow.

"Did you say Raeburn?"

"Yes — four Willow Terrace is the address."

Hal gasped.

"I don't believe it! Fancy Louise Raeburn's niece walking into your life like that."

"Who is Louise Raeburn?" Scott was bewildered.

A COUNTRY CHRISTMAS EVE

WE are ready; waiting to depart. By the doorway, before the night's dark mouth.

Fields are dressed in frost; ice upon the pond looks milky.

A thin young moon is long since bedded; the glittering stars are all awake.

We listen – Ah, there it is now!

Sound of the bell from the auld kirk steeple; clear, distant from across the valley.

As sound the bells of Bethlehem in Christ's own native land, so rings the summons from a rural belfry.

To take the country road, and reach a local Angus Bethlehem.

As sounds the voice of God through the dark of this benighted world, so speaks of God the auld kirk bell.

"Come ye . . . come ye . . . come ye to me!"

Rev. T. R. S. Campbell.

"Someone I'd have married if your grandmother hadn't come along."

"Well, if she's anything like her niece," Scott replied, "I don't blame you for dropping her!"

Hal wagged a disapproving finger.

"I'll hear nothing bad about Louise. She was a fine woman, but long before your grandmother came into my life, Louise and I were falling out. She was keener to marry than I was at that moment."

Hal laughed.

"I was a wild laddie then, rather like you are now. I didn't want to settle down. You see, with Louise and I growing up together, we were just too close, almost smothering each other.

"That's why I wasn't sure whether marriage to Louise would work. She didn't agree with me, so we gradually drifted apart."

He sighed, remembering.

"Then your grandmother came into my life and I knew she was the one. My feelings for her were completely different from the ones I had for Louise, who was my first love." He paused thoughtfully. "Your gran and I were happy, but you never forget your first romance."

"Pamela says her aunt's retired now and missing her work terribly. Surely you could call on an old friend."

"Thanks for trying to help, but I've made up my mind. There's no going back."

Scott wondered if he really meant that, bringing to mind his grandfather's recent outburst about storing up grief.

Could that have had anything to do with Louise Raeburn? More importantly, was Pamela's aunt the reason for her coolness? Did Pamela know the story about the break-up and was she blaming the Lindsays?

If so, what chance was there for any friendship between them?

PAMELA RAEBURN felt utterly confused at why she should take her spite out on Scott Lindsay. What had he to do with a disagreement that took place years ago? She wanted desperately to talk to him, to open her heart, but would she ever have the opportunity?

Loyalty to Aunt Louise had kept her away from the workshop to inquire about the desk. Now, she was nervously clutching the postcard telling her the desk was finished, and was on her way to make arrangements for its delivery to Willow Terrace.

Pam steeled herself for the meeting with Scott but was faced instead by Hal Lindsay. Her impressions were of a tall, proud man, grey haired, not at all like the ogre she'd imagined had let her aunt down all those years ago.

"You'll be Pamela, Miss Raeburn's niece. Scott's spoken a lot about you. He's not here at the moment, but you'll be wanting to see the desk."

She followed him into the workshop.

"And how's your aunt these days?"

"She's well, Mr Lindsay, but time's tending to drag now she's home all day."

"Well, Miss Raeburn, what d'you think?" he asked, indicating the desk.

"Super!" Pam enthused. "Aunt Louise will be delighted. She's very fond of this old desk."

"All Scott's work," he told her proudly. "With a wee bit of my advice thrown in."

He wasn't slow to notice the admiration in her eyes at the mention of Scott's name. She was so like Louise had been when she was young. Just to glance at her was enough to make his heart turn over. He'd had the same feeling when Scott had removed the back of the desk and found an old, faded letter jammed inside written in his neat handwriting.

Now, looking at Pamela, he wondered whether he should return it to Louise or just destroy it.

JUST then, Scott returned and, noticing the change of expression on Pamela's face, Hal made an excuse to leave. It could only be knowledge of the past which was keeping them apart, and he didn't want to feel responsible for that.

Pam looked hesitatingly at Scott.

"You've made a lovely job of the desk. My aunt will be pleased."

"Thanks."

"Your grandfather's pleased with your work."

"I'm glad — he's a hard taskmaster."

Their conversation was stilted, uncomfortable. It drifted away till there was nothing left to do but stare at each other anxiously.

"I'd love to get to know you better, Pam," Scott said. "And I know the very place to start — a pleasant little bistro, not far from here."

"Say no more!" Pam sighed. "Let's fix a time."

In the relaxed atmosphere of the restaurant and each other's company, words came easily.

"I've tried to persuade my grandfather to visit your aunt, but he'd rather be lonely than upset her," Scott confided.

"But what can we do?" Pamela asked.

"Very little," Scott replied. "I hope something happens before I deliver the desk. After that, there'll be no point of contact between them. And our friendship won't be complete until they settle their differences. We'll always be inclined to take sides."

HAL LINDSAY hovered nervously outside the gate of four Willow Terrace, at last plucking up courage to go in.

How will Louise greet me, he asked himself.

But she was calmness itself and welcomed him warmly. They sat in the bay window overlooking the immaculately-kept garden.

He'd rehearsed his speech all the way along the road and suddenly the words came tumbling out, thoughts about the past, how stupid they'd been.

"Just because we made fools of ourselves," he finished, "doesn't seem reason to spoil anything for our young people."

Louise's reply was sharp in its rebuke.

"Hal Lindsay, you come to my house after all these years without so much as a greeting, and lecture me about my niece's future."

Hal's shoulders slumped.

"I didn't mean to hurt your feelings, but when I saw them, daggers drawn, because of me, I knew something had to be done."

He stood up. "Well, I've made a mess of this, haven't I? I'll leave now before anything else is said."

"Hal Lindsay, sit down this minute and listen to me because I happen to agree with you!" She smiled. "You always were soft hearted."

Hal gave a rueful smile.

"D'you know what gave me the courage to come here? This."

He gave her the letter with its faded handwriting, explaining where he'd found it.

"And I thought I'd destroyed them all," she murmured. "Then it wasn't just the young people's welfare that brought you here?"

Hal's mouth lifted into a half smile.

"I never could fool you, Louise, and I've been so lonely since Emily died. I wanted to come but I was scared of intruding."

"Oh, Hal! Since I retired I haven't known what to do with myself. I've mooned about the house, never settling. I needed someone like you to talk some sense into me."

At that moment, the blackness of the past was dissolving away.

"What about the future, Louise?"

She sighed.

"Obviously, marriage wasn't for us, Hal — we'd have driven each other daft! But we can always be friends. Maybe we'll see in the young folk what we might have been. At least we can make sure we do the right thing by them, giving them our blessing."

Suddenly they were laughing, and when it had died down, Louise held up the letter.

"What would you say if I were to drop this letter in the fire, Hal?"

"I'd say good riddance! A few words on a piece of paper, written years ago, have served their purpose and brought me back to you."

As the letter blackened and curled into ashes, Pamela and Scott came in, both looking delighted.

"Scott, I've been thinking," Hal said. "You've made such a good job of Louise's desk, that there might be a spark of responsibility in you after all. I'm sure you won't mind if I spend a bit more time away from the shop, will you? After all, I've got to get used to retirement when it comes, and Louise has been at a loose end since she retired."

Scott was taken by surprise, but responded when Pamela dug him with an elbow.

"You take as much time off as you like, Grandad," he blurted out. Then he took Pam's hand . . . "It's been quite a day, hasn't it? Lindsays and Raeburns together again, both young and old!" □

The ruins of Kelso Abbey are a great architectural attraction, having been founded as early as 1128 by David I. In the twelfth century, Kelso, now a busy market town, had its fair share of suffering at the hands of the English. Several treaties between the Scots and the English were also arranged here. When, in 1545, the Earl of Hertford entered Kelso, the abbey was garrisoned as a fortress and taken at the point of the sword. From 1649 till 1771 the existing transept was used as a parish church, but in 1805 the unsightly additions were removed and in 1919 it was presented to the nation.

KELSO ABBEY : J CAMPBELL KERR

TO walk down the only street in Cromult takes about ten minutes. A small village, it has only twelve houses and a straggle of tiny shops, yet the spot is very popular with tourists and, as soon as the season begins, the narrow cobbled street is packed with cars.

One spring day, when the trees were freshly green, and the birds were searching for sites to built their nests, Sam Polly stood outside his emporium and took a long hard look at his property. Then turned to Amy Brown, who ran The Newsbox next door.

"Do you think Joe Wainwright is correct? Our shops do look a bit old-fashioned."

Amy Brown gazed up at the questioner. She had to look up, for Sam was six feet in the stocking soles, and she just a diminutive five.

"Not at all" she returned stoutly, "The Polly, and my Newsbox wouldn't look right all shiny and covered in plastic."

Joe Wainwright, the grocer, three along, had just installed a new frontage. His property had been boarded up for two weeks and Sam and Amy listened curiously to the sounds of muffled hammering as the shopfitters from the city completed the transformation.

Then, when the boarding was removed, Joe's brand-new image was revealed for all to see. Villagers and passers-by alike flocked to admire the bright new premises.

Wainwright for bargains announced a red slash of paper pasted across Joe's plate-glass window, and another, *Free gift for first twenty customers.*

There had been a queue outside the shop since eight that morning, but it wasn't just the free gift scheme that worried Sam, but the fact that the new front seemed to put his own property in the shade — and Amy's too.

The emporium and the newsagents, having adjoining properties, had always kept their decor alike — dark wood panelling with the lettering above the doors traced out in old gold. Compared to Joe's shiny white frontage they did seem rather dull.

Amy and Sam had been friends all their lives. It was nothing for Amy to store half a dozen rolls of linoleum in her back shop, if Sam happened to have gone up to the city warehouse when the van arrived.

Likewise, Sam would rise at five each morning and drive the five miles to the nearest railway station to collect her newspapers. But then, in the trade, such co-operation was taken for granted.

After the shopfitters had left, Joe Wainwright had hurried down the street to where Sam and Amy were standing.

"Don't you think it's time you two joined the twentieth century?" he'd remarked.

Sam and Amy had disdained making any comment, and Joe had watched as Sam began his daily ritual, which was to carry outside a selection of his wares for his pavement display.

First, came the clothes baskets filled with oddments, then a selection of aluminium pails, a garden hose and, last of all, a petrol-driven lawn-mower.

Earlier, while Sam had been waiting for the train to arrive, a fisherman

Put The Kettle On, Mrs Polly

by Ailie Scullion

had sold him two dozen sea urchin shells, and these he'd hung in a string net just above his door, where customers could see them the moment they walked inside.

"Who wants to buy seashells?" Joe had asked, watching as Sam doggedly continued to work.

"Haven't you anything better to do with your time, Joe Wainwright?" Amy had demanded sharply.

The grocer hadn't been in the least put out.

"Take a look along the street, Amy my love. There's a queue outside my shop, but I don't see any at yours. Keep 'em waiting, is my motto."

Sam gave a grunt as he placed a box of geraniums below his window. Amy had also began to display her wares outside. Coloured postcards clipped into a rack which she hung outside her door. Then there was the roly-poly man advertising ice-cream, and of course the stop press poster to be displayed.

"Why don't you take your counters out on to the pavement and be done with it?" Joe commented. He seemed determined to rub salt into the wound, but Amy was ready for him.

"Why don't you run along, Joe," she told him sweetly, "and give away your free sausages? If they're anything like the ones I bought from you last week the customers are welcome. Full of breadcrumbs they were."

A MY'S last comment did the trick. The grocer swung round on his heel and left. Sam and Amy stared after him.

"Don't bother about that wee grocer," Amy consoled Sam now, "our shops are fine the way they are."

Sam agreed half-heartedly, but was not too convinced, and later, after it grew dark, he took a stroll along to take a better look at Joe's shop. He had to admit the place looked smart — hygienic, too.

Sam jumped as he heard a voice behind him.

"Taking another look, are you, Sam?"

The grocer must have crept up behind him. Sam could have kicked himself for having been caught out.

"Don't worry," Joe assured him now. "I understand you and Amy must be feeling a bit put out, but we're all business folk, and should help one another. Tell you what, Sam, I'll let you have the name of my shopfitter."

He produced a business card from his waistcoat pocket.

Sam hurried back to Amy's flat to show it to her.

"I don't know." She spoke doubtfully. "Of course, it's up to you, but I can't see all that plastic and white paint suiting us. I mean, our shops have become almost institutions in Cromult. Customers wouldn't feel the same if we made them look like ice-cream parlours."

He mulled over Amy's advice as he sat down to his plate of steak and kidney pie. Amy always made this on Thursday evenings. It had become the highlight of Sam's week.

"No use me baking for one," she'd explain. "Come up and have a bite after the Polly is shut."

Put The Kettle On, Mrs Polly

Theirs was rather a unique sort of relationship. Sam and Amy were of an age, Sam being forty-five, Amy, three years his junior. Of course they should have been married years ago, but always something had stopped him proposing.

For one thing, until a year ago they both had responsibilities. His mother was still alive, and he felt it wouldn't be right for Amy to share a home with another woman. Then there was Amy's dad — a fine man he was too, but hadn't left his bed in ten years.

Mr Brown had died shortly after his own mother, but by then Sam, it seemed, had developed cold feet, and couldn't pluck up courage to ask that important question.

But she was a wonderful person, Sam realised fondly, such a generous nature she possessed. He couldn't ever remember having a cross word with her.

THAT night he wrote away to Shipman Wrights, Joe's shopfitters, and asked for some brochures. It would do no harm to look at them, he supposed.

But, when their representative arrived one week later, Sam got the shock of his life, for it was no high-powered salesman with a bushy moustache and bulging briefcase.

Janice Cowper looked just like one of the model girls who adorned the front covers of Amy's coloured magazines. She was slender as a wand and tall, almost reaching Sam's shoulder, and her hair was either fair or red, but whatever, it shone in the early-morning sun as she approached him with a slim hand extended.

They talked for a while about mundane matters, such as the prettiness of Cromult village and how the tourist season would soon be hotting up, then Janice decided to get down to business.

"Perhaps we could step outside for a moment, so we can discuss which style would be most suitable for your emporium."

"I haven't really decided whether to go ahead . . ." he began, but she was already moving towards the door, and he followed, head bowed like an obedient spaniel, and joined her on the pavement.

"Ah, yes," Janice spoke confidently. "I do believe our de luxe finish is what you require. But let me show you the designs, Sam."

She leaned across, her head close to his, and he could smell a heady perfume as she flicked over a pile of coloured illustrations. But Sam hardly took them in, for he'd become conscious of the fact that Amy was standing in her doorway watching this performance.

"Yes, definitely the de luxe model, cream fascia with teak surrounds. A bit more expensive, but well worth the difference. Of course, we would have to get rid of all that clutter."

Sam looked slightly hurt as Janice pointed towards his pavement display.

"You have to admit, advertising the way you are approaching it, Sam, is a bit outdated. Modern promotions such as Mr Wainwright employs is what will liven up your trade."

"A free sea urchin with every can of paraffin," Amy said just loudly enough for Sam to hear, then she turned and disappeared into her shop.

Amy's remark had been a bit uncalled for, he decided. After all, Joe had told him only this morning that his "free gift" gimmick had worked so well, he'd decided to continue it all week. Today's offer was a can of cream with every punnet of imported strawberries sold.

"Well?" Janice asked, after they sat down together for lunch in the Stag's Head. "Are you pleased that you've taken the plunge?"

Sam was very aware of the attractive sales rep. sitting opposite, especially her long slim legs which she had crossed so elegantly, but he was aware too, of the curious stares of locals who were watching the scene.

It had seemed only fair to take the girl out to lunch, after all her hard work this morning. In actual fact, it was really Sam who had done the hard work, moving all that pavement display. She'd merely supervised until the pavement was bare and even the racks attached to his window-sill removed, exposing the faded varnish underneath.

"Oh dear." She had sighed then. "The place certainly does need a face-lift."

Sam had had to agree.

Now, as she tucked into a plate of lasagne, Sam stole an admiring glance at his companion. Fancy someone so young and beautiful as Janice, turning out to be so persuasive.

He could hardly believe that she'd got him to sign up for the 'full treatment.' The price had been staggering, but he wouldn't think of that now.

Anyway, Janice had assured him that he would recoup this with increased trade.

It was only when Janice brought her name up, that Sam remembered Amy.

"Once the emporium has been renovated, I'm afraid it will show up that dreadful shop next door. Tell me, Sam, do you have any influence with Miss Brown? She wasn't terribly helpful when I called in."

Sam raised one dark eyebrow. He had not been aware that Janice had called in at the Newsbox. It must have been when he went upstairs to collect his cheque book.

A Woman's Reasons

THE things I love you for are little things —
Your gentle hands; your rarely-tidy tie;
Your sudden smile; the way you touch my cheek;
The teasing glint of mischief in your eye.

I love the way you laugh; your easy stride;
The habit that you have — you'd never guess!
Of rumpling up your hair. Such foolish things,
But oh, they touch my heart to tenderness!

Claire Ritchie.

Then he remembered something else. It was Thursday, and Amy hadn't invited him over for tea.

"Tell you what," Janice broke into his thoughts, "I have some other lines across at the hotel. Perhaps if you'd join me for dinner tonight, I could let you have some samples, then you could show them to your neighbour, persuade her to change her mind. However, I very much doubt it. Miss Brown is a very stubborn lady."

Sam felt he should speak up for Amy, especially when Janice began to talk about backward-thinking retailers who refused to move with the times.

"Amy . . . I mean, Miss Brown, has led a rather difficult life, Janice. Her father was an invalid for many years and she nursed him until he died."

"I know the type," the girl opposite broke in, "salt of the earth, but with absolutely no imagination."

Later, when he did speak to Amy, she was quite adamant that she wanted none of Janice Cowper's improvements in her shop, and made it clear that she strongly disapproved of Sam's own plans.

"What would your father say, Sam Polly, if he were to come back and see what you intended to do with the emporium? And anyway, what does a young girl like that know about shops such as ours?"

She looked questioningly at Sam.

"This isn't the big city, you know. Besides, one of the main attractions for tourists is our 'quaint little shops,' as your Miss Cowper puts it. And as for taking away your pavement display, I just hope you don't live to regret it."

Sam was hurt by her attitude, and after a few more curt exchanges he turned on his heel.

A FTER that, Sam and Amy kept out of each other's way as much as possible. Sam still collected the newspapers each morning though, and stacked them neatly outside Amy's door.

Before their disagreement, if the morning was a cold one, Amy would throw up the window on his return, and invite Sam up for breakfast. Bacon and eggs always tasted better when Amy cooked them.

He hadn't received such an invitation all week, and this morning, it had been so cold that he'd had to pull up his collar to stop himself from shivering.

But it was his chats with Amy that he missed most of all.

Sam had seen nothing of Janice Cowper either, since she'd spoken to him the previous week. He rang her firm to enquire when the work was likely to commence on his shop, and the man on the line said that it would be July or August.

"But that will be in the height of my season," he blurted out. "I couldn't possible close 'The Polly' then."

"Sorry," the man said in a disinterested voice. "July and August are the only dates available."

Sam frowned into the receiver. It seemed that whenever these people collected their deposit, they lost interest in their customers.

After he closed his shop and went upstairs to open a tin of sausages and beans, Sam went to gaze out of the window.

It was a lovely evening. The sun was about to set over Gowrie Brae. He decided to go for a walk. Normally, when he planned to do this, he'd have called in at Amy's, and suggest that she join him, but things being as they were, he set out alone.

When he reached the reservoir, high above Cromult, Sam stopped for breath beside the Stone Well. Above the ancient iron tap a brass plate had been set into the wall and on it was printed a verse:

> *Here's the bonnie wee well*
> *at the breist o' the brae,*
> *where the birds dip their beaks*
> *in the heat o' the day . . .*

How often they would stand at this well and recite the verse. Then Sam would fill the iron cup with the clear mountain water and watch as Amy drank, one small finger placed along the edge of the iron cup.

How he missed his Amy, and her small smooth face, her warm natural laughter, and the feel of her tiny cold hand which he'd wrap inside his own, then tuck them both inside his coat pocket as they walked back down the hill.

S AM filled the iron cup with water and was about to drink when he heard the voice behind him:

"Here's the bonnie wee well at the breist o' the brae . . ."

He wheeled around.

"Oh, Amy! Amy, Amy, Amy."

He repeated her name over and over again, savouring the word as his eyes took on her familiar face. She had been sitting on the old wrought-iron seat which was half hidden among the elderberry bushes. The villagers called it "lovers' seat" because it was to this destination most courting couples found their way of an evening.

He sat down quickly by her side.

"I thought you'd never arrive," she admitted frankly, "I've been tramping up here every night this week."

He should have known! When they were younger, after any slight disagreement, they would walk up Gowrie's Brae, drink some of the healing water and make up. This they did now.

"I was wrong," Sam admitted, winding his long arm around Amy's waist. "It was greed, of course. It was when the girl talked about doubling my profits; as if I didn't have a good enough turnover!"

He smiled at her.

"And you were right, Amy, I've no stomach for turning the Polly into an ice-cream parlour, and I miss my mops and buckets out on the pavement. First thing tomorrow, they're going back out. I'll write and cancel the contract and to hang with the deposit. It will be cheap at the price."

One thing about his Amy, she had never been one to hold on to a grievance, and with her head pressed against his chest, she suddenly looked up.

"Joe was right about one thing, however, Sam. Our shops do need a face-lift — but in moderation."

He nodded happily.

"Oh, there are going to be changes all right, Amy, my pet. I can promise you that."

CROMULT'S tourist season was again in full swing. The narrow street was crowded with summer-clad tourists.

"Such a darling little place," an American lady announced to her camera-snapping husband. "And would you look at that cute name above the door?"

Polly's Emporium it read, and underneath *(incorporating Amy's Newsbox)*. Bright new varnish gleamed between the racks of coloured magazines. On the pavement, were some aluminium pails filled to the brim with bright-coloured beach balls.

Inside the shop, an intervening wall had been removed so that there was a wide floorage for customers to browse.

Mrs Polly still sold her newspapers from her own personal counter, but she had absolutely no objection to lending a hand in the emporium whenever the rush for newsprint was over. And she never bored of listening to her husband's standing joke whenever there was a lull in trade.

"Mrs Polly!" he would call across the shop. "Put the kettle on."

Obligingly, she would run upstairs to do as she was bid. Such a lovely apartment they now had, since the flats had been knocked into one.

As she handed Sam his cup, he bent low and kissed the top of her head.

"Happy, Mrs Polly?"

Amy nodded her head.

"Never happier, Sam."

He glanced up at the clock. It showed half-past five. It was time to begin. Of one accord, they were galvanised into activity. In came the roly-poly man, the clothes baskets, then Sam pulled down the shutters and took in the striped sun awnings.

As the two of them returned and Sam bolted the door, and switched the "Open" card to "Closed," he turned to his wife.

"Ay, Amy, we might be a bit old-fashioned, at least according to Joe Wainwright, but I can't say it has reflected on our profits, eh, love?"

She nodded her agreement.

"I hear Joe has stopped his give-aways. His wife told me it was running away with their profit."

"Poor Joe!" Sam really meant that too, for he didn't mind being considered old-fashioned, and anyway, right now, he felt anything but staid.

"Upstairs then, Mrs Polly," he said in a masterful voice.

Amy smiled mischievously as she took off the blue shop overall with its slogan — "Polly's for a square deal." Then she turned, like the dutiful wife that she was.

"Coming, Mr Polly!" she said demurely. □

SANTA'S SPECIAL

By Laura Caldwell

RUTH LYLE mounted the steps to fix a spray of holly over the picture of Jesus and the children.

It was a favourite picture. The boys and girls of Knox House loved it because it was full of bright colours and happy faces of every colour and race. *Suffer the little children to come unto me,* ran the inscription below the picture.

Jesus was smiling too, his eyes shining warm and kind, his arms held out to shelter the children. What would happen to the picture now?

From her perch Ruth looked down on the spacious room. What would happen to the stout old table, made to seat twenty children and more? What would happen to the bookcase overflowing with children's books, the bulging games cupboard, the rocking-horse? Where would the toys be by next Christmas? Where would she, Ruth Lyle, be next Christmas?

The loaded question brought momentary panic to the slight, young girl. Next Christmas was an unknown quantity.

Last Christmas there had been the pain of losing Martin. After a whole year together, Martin Laing had found someone else; someone with money.

"One has to be realistic, Ruth, poppet," he'd told her. "A bit of capital's just what's desperately needed in this new project I want to get going."

Ruth could hardly believe it. How was it possible to have loved so blindly, not knowing what Martin was really like?

The shock of their break-up had had a traumatic effect on young Ruth. It had made her grow up suddenly. From now on she'd be wary.

If men could swear they loved you one minute and then with a snap of the fingers simply cancel it all out, leaving you emotionally shattered, then she would certainly not run the risk of falling in love again.

After a week of tears and misery, Ruth had pulled herself together and looked around for a change of scene, a change of job.

She searched for something that would fill her days with hard work, a caring job that would be worth doing well and would make her forget Martin Laing.

She found exactly that as assistant matron in a home for deprived children, and had moved from London to Knox House in the small Galloway market town of Caddum.

RUTH came down from her perch and stood back to view her decorations; holly and mistletoe, silver stars along the mantelpiece, a scarlet paper chain looped round the walls.

GIFT

konradsen

Then she went to draw the curtains, shutting out the bare trees and empty lawns. Next Christmas there would only be a heap of rubble where Knox House now stood. Serious dry-rot had been discovered in the Victorian mansion and the powers-that-be had decided to demolish it.

Since late autumn the small children had been gradually leaving. A home of their own, with loving families, had been found for most of them. By late November only three little boys remained. Of course, the staff had dwindled too, leaving to find work elsewhere. Now, there was just Ruth, and big Ivor Halliday.

The Rev. Cyril Munn, chairman of the home's board of governors, had telephoned Ruth a week ago.

"Any happy news for the Bruce boys?" He had tried to make his voice sound light.

"No, nothing," Ruth had had to confess.

"Well, we must just go on hoping. Some good people will surely come along; a couple who . . . who feel . . ." The minister was finding it difficult to put into words the special problems presented by the Bruce brothers.

Ruth, too, was worried about them.

"What will happen, Mr Munn? I mean, if the boys are not adopted what will happen when Knox House closes?"

"Nothing terrible, Ruth, I can promise you that. Places will be found for them in other homes."

Other homes? That meant a transfer to Glasgow, far away from the school-chums they had made here in the friendly Galloway community. And would they still be together? This question nagged at Ruth these days. Would the three wee brothers be kept together?

IT'S because there are *three* of them," the Rev. Munn explained to his committee. "People will eagerly adopt one child, a few are to be found who will welcome two, but *three!*"

The committee were silent. They all knew that this was the stumbling block. They all knew too that Hughie Bruce, who was barely five, was — well, to put it mildly, *difficult* these days.

"I try, but lately I can't get a word out of the child. It's as if he'd lost the power to speak. How do you cope with this, Ruth?"

"Hughie has always been quiet, and lately he's become much worse. But he's a darling child just the same."

Ruth's kind heart bled for the Bruce family. She knew wee Hughie was a problem. She knew, too, that various parents would have taken Kit and Willie Bruce, given them a loving home; but nine-year-old Kit had dug in his heels.

"Willie an' me's no' going anywhere without wee Hughie." And the eldest Bruce brother would not budge one inch from that decision.

That afternoon the minister had a serious talk with Kit.

"Some other kind parents will welcome wee Hughie on his own," he'd told him. "Maybe someone living in Galloway, in Caddum even, so that you would all see each other quite often." He went on to warn

Kit. "By being so obstinate you might be depriving your little brother of a happy home life."

Kit was an intelligent youngster. He thought about all that Mr Munn had said. Then he sounded his little brother. But wee Hughie's blue eyes clouded over, he clamped his mouth tight shut and wouldn't say a word.

But that night, in the dark, when the boys were tucked up in the nearly empty dormitory, Hughie's voice miraculously came back.

"Are you listening, Kit? I don't want to go to anyone's house. I don't want to go anywhere without you and Willie. D'ye hear me Kit? Please."

"It's all right, you won't have to, Hughie. I've told you before, we're a *family*; you an' me an' Willie, we're the Bruce family! Nobody's goin' to do anything to us, hear that? Now shut up and go to sleep, for Pete's sake." Kit was acting the exasperated big brother, but his child's heart trembled for wee Hughie, and Willie.

R UTH finished fixing the sprays of bright holly Ivor Halliday had brought her that morning fresh from the woods around Knox House. Then she set out the roughly-carved Christmas scene; Mary and Joseph and the baby in the manger, the three kings, the shepherds, the donkeys, the lambs.

Ruth was determined to make this Christmas as it had always been for the children of Knox House, a happy time, bright with hope.

She had decided against having the usual giant Christmas tree. Over the years the boys and girls had been allowed to decorate the tree from the box of tinsel and miniature toys.

But this Christmas there would only be the wee Bruce brothers and herself and big Ivor. A giant of a tree would look all wrong. Yet now, as she looked round the room, it did seem to her something was missing . . . maybe she'd been too quick in telling Ivor not to bring one in.

Ruth glanced at her watch. Half past six already! The boys would be back at seven. They had gone to the church to practise carols for Christmas Eve. They'd be clamouring for hot chocolate and gingerbread before bed.

Ruth went through to the kitchen to prepare supper.

It was a wild night. The wind was howling through the trees outside and rattling at the windows of the old house. Then, above the wind another sound came to her ears. Crunch, crunch on the gravel path, and then a muffled knocking at the kitchen window.

London-bred, Ruth had taken a long time to grow accustomed to a country life; at first she had found the silence around Knox House disturbing.

Every sound, like the wind and rain, or heavy footsteps, seemed exaggerated. Now her heart began to thump. She pulled aside a curtain — then screamed aloud. A darkly-bearded face weirdly surrounded by a mass of greenery was staring in at her.

In a moment the face had broken into a wide grin. Ruth's fears vanished. She shook her small fist at the laughing young man outside.

"That wasn't funny," she raged, "not at all funny, Ivor Halliday!"

She had a good mind not to open the door. But Ivor was burdened by a tree, a wide-branched Christmas tree. When he came in with it the wind at once slammed the door shut.

"Some night!" Ivor said.

"Why did you scare me like that?" Ruth demanded angrily.

"I guess I was a little bit afraid . . ."

"You afraid! It was me who got the fright."

"Aw, that was nothing, Ruth. I mean I was afraid to bring in the tree. I know you didn't want one this year. But I came on this little fellow on the edge of the woods. I couldn't resist it, he's a real beauty. And see this, I've kept the roots OK."

It was, indeed, a very pretty little tree, just the right size for three children. Ruth's heart soon melted.

"But never frighten me like that again, Ivor. Do you hear, never!"

"Right, ma'am. Real sorry, ma'am, honestly, ma'am." And big Ivor bobbed and touched his forelock.

"And don't be cheeky. You're worse than the boys. Now fetch the green pail, you can set up the tree in that."

IVOR HALLIDAY and Ruth Lyle had worked together for the past twelve months and felt easy in each other's company.

At the same time they knew very little about each other. And that was the way it must stay, Ruth had decided. For hadn't she promised herself no more emotional entanglements?

To date, all Ruth knew about big Ivor was that he had come to work at Knox House around the same time as she had; that he was from Canada and was quite the best man-about-the-house any board of governors could wish for.

Ivor set up the little Christmas tree now, and Ruth had just fetched the box of decorations when the three Bruce boys arrived back.

"The minister gave us a lift home," Kit explained. "And he says to tell you that he might look in on Christmas Day."

Might look in on Christmas Day! Ruth smiled. She knew that Christmas Day would be pretty flat if the Rev. Cyril Munn didn't look in! For he appeared as Santa Claus year after year, arriving with a clatter of hooves and ringing bells, much to the joy of the Knox House children.

Ruth knelt to unfasten wee Hughie's winter coat.

"And have you all the carols off pat for Christmas Eve, love?" she asked the little boy. But Hughie put his head down and wouldn't answer.

"He never sang at all, Ruth. Hughie just wouldn't sing. Honest, you get sick of him never talking, so you do. Someone should punch his nose *hard.*" Willie, the middle Bruce brother, drank his hot chocolate with a great deal of noise to express his exasperation.

"If you punch wee Hughie's nose I'll punch yours, Willie Bruce. I'll make your head birl like a peerie and turn your nose into jelly!" And Kit faced Willie, his face red, his fists raised.

"Stop this, stop it!" Ruth cried, pulling the brothers apart. "I'll have no fighting at Christmas time. Shame on you, Willie."

At bedtime Ruth always had a special wee hug for Hughie. The small, pale boy tore at her heart and brought out all the loving mothering instincts in Ruth Lyle.

As the weeks had gone by, Hughie and his brothers and their plight had made her own upset over Martin Laing seem paltry in comparison.

The truth was Ruth's work among the deprived children had wrought a small miracle. The hurt Martin had done her was fading. She was kept so busy that one day overflowed into the next. Though, lately, so near the end for Knox House, a chill had crept into her heart. What now for the three small boys? What now for herself?

A S she saw the pyjama-clad children upstairs to bed, the chill welled up in her again. In the big room the wee brothers seemed smaller than ever; they appeared so vulnerable, so alone. She heard their prayers, then added a little silent one herself.

*Please, God – no, please, **Jesus** who loves all children so much, find a loving home for Tom and Willie and wee Hughie. Please, please, Jesus, at Christmas time, make these little boys know what happiness is. Amen.*

By the time she'd tucked them up, with kisses all round, the chill of fear, for the moment at least, had miraculously gone.

On her way downstairs she collided with Ivor who was dashing up three steps at a time to look in at the dormitory and say goodnight. Ruth literally fell into his arms. But Ivor didn't release her immediately. Instead, his hold tightened. She was conscious of his strong hands holding her, and conscious too that close contact with the handsome young Canadian caused her heart-beat to quicken.

Ivor's lips sought hers. His kiss was demanding, wafting Ruth out of time and into space.

He had kissed her before, but just in a light-hearted, teasing way. This was very different.

Then, without warning, there drifted into Ruth's mind a picture of Martin Laing.

Martin's kisses had once been wonderful, hadn't they? And yet she knew now they could have meant nothing, nothing at all, to Martin!

Her reaction to such thoughts was swift; she wriggled free of Ivor's tight hold. She was aware of his disappointment, his puzzled expression.

"What's wrong?" he asked almost angrily. "Surely you're not scared of me?"

Then he regained his composure.

"Sorry. I must have lost my head for a moment. Maybe it's because it's Christmas; maybe it's the season for spreading love around."

He went quickly on up the stairs.

Ruth felt humiliated, upset that she had handled the little incident so clumsily. What an immature little fool Ivor must think her. Well, what if he did! Ivor Halliday was nothing to her. No man meant anything to her any more. Wasn't that how she wanted it? *Wasn't it?*

L ATER Ruth and Ivor had supper together. The meal began in silence, but soon the young Canadian began to talk.

"You got any news of a new job, Ruth?"

Ruth was more relieved than she cared to admit that he was friendly again. She shook her head.

"I keep on applying. I'm waiting for word now about one. What about you, Ivor?"

"I'm waiting for a letter too."

"About a job?"

Ivor was quite a time in answering.

"Not exactly . . . but in a sense yes. I'm waiting for a letter from my father in Ontario. I want to get home, I want to work for him again." The words came out in a rush.

So, Ruth thought, Ivor does have a family. And it struck her how little she knew about him.

Now that they were so soon to part, go their own ways, she felt a kind of panic. Maybe she should have shown more interest in Ivor. But Martin's treatment of her had made her over sensitive.

"If no mail comes for me by Christmas Day then I guess I won't be going back at all," Ivor was continuing. His fingers were playing tensely with the narrow hyde thong he wore around his neck.

Ruth had never seen Ivor without the necklet. She had noticed that it ended only in a twisted metal ring. Why did Ivor wear such a shabby ornament? Had it some special meaning?

But Ruth was not ready to probe into that yet.

"What's it like where you come from, Ivor?" she asked, instead. She could see the unhappiness in his eyes and instinctively wanted to comfort him.

"Ontario? Well, right now the snow will be knee-high in our town and the lake frozen hard. Main Street will be bursting out with coloured lanterns, and the Halliday Christmas tree — a huge affair in silver dotted with lit-up golden apples — will be shining at the entrance to

Orchard Acres. That's the name of my home, Ruth, Orchard Acres.''

"It's a lovely name."

"Every Christmas since I was a little fellow, my dad set up a giant of a tree for the folk to enjoy." Ivor was laughing a little, shaking his head as if he couldn't quite believe it all.

"They say some folk were born with a silver spoon in their mouths. Was that you, Ivor?"

"Yeah, I guess it just about fits me. Only I was born with a solid gold apple in mine! My grandfather and my father are head of the Orchard Acres Apple Corporation."

"Lucky you!" Ruth smiled. But what happened, Ivor, she wanted to ask. Why aren't you in Ontario now, working in the family business? What went wrong? But she wouldn't let herself voice the questions. Aloud she just repeated: "Lucky you, Ivor!"

To her astonishment, Ivor Halliday shook his head emphatically.

"Lucky me? No, I don't go along with that any more. You know something, all the years I was growing up I was at the receiving end. I took it all for granted." He shrugged.

"My lifestyle was geared that way. I had only to express a wish for something — a motor cycle, a speedboat on the lake, later fast cars and plenty of so-called friends to share the fun with me — and it was mine!

Gems

SOMEONE to listen,
Someone to cheer,
Somewhere a shoulder
When shedding a tear.
Somewhere the kindness
To help us in need,
Gems to be treasured
Of friendship indeed!

Elizabeth Gozney.

"But that's no good, Ruth. That kind of boyhood doesn't make for true happiness. In fact, probably the wisest thing my father ever did for me was . . ."

At that moment, out in the hall, the phone began to shrill and Ruth had to jump up to answer it.

"Good evening, Ruth, my dear." It was the Rev. Cyril Munn. "Look, I've an invitation for the Bruce boys. It's for a children's party after the carol-singing on Christmas Eve. I must have your permission, of course. George and Dolly Ramsay are inviting all the youngsters. I understand it's going to be quite a 'do'! No less a V.I.P. than Santa Claus is to be present! They've persuaded one of the hotel guests to take that part!" The kindly minister chuckled.

The Ramsays were hosts at the Market Inn, Caddum's only hotel.

"I'll see them safely home, of course," Mr Munn assured Ruth. She was delighted for her boys.

When she returned to the kitchen Ivor Halliday was already on his feet, winding his absurdly-long scarf around his neck.

"I'll get going. Thanks for the supper . . . and, Ruth, thanks for listening! See you tomorrow."

THAT night Ruth couldn't get the thought of Ivor Halliday out of her head. She could easily picture him in just such a setting as Orchard Acres. Then what was he doing here, in a remote corner of Scotland working for what amounted to just pocket money? This was a mystery. Ruth fell asleep still puzzling over it.

Ivor returned to his cottage in the woods. He felt wide awake. It had been great to talk to Ruth. "*Ruth.*" He whispered the name aloud. It suited so well her special quiet beauty. How was he to face up to the idea he might soon never see her again?

He threw a log on the dying fire and watched bright sparks exploding up the chimney. But the fire-pictures didn't dispel his crowding problems.

Why had his father not acknowledged his letter? Even a Christmas card would have been better than nothing. Maybe it had got lost? But Ivor knew that mail very seldom went missing.

His troubled thoughts went back now to Ontario, to Orchard Acres, to his years at college. Ivor had made a fool of himself, he'd been ready for a long time to admit that.

Now, in the quiet of the cottage, he looked back on the final traumatic row between him and his father. He remembered Gus Halliday's bitter tirade over the misdeeds of his only son — the wasted time at college, the classes frequently skipped, the wrong friends, the shattering failure in his final exams. And, what was the last straw to his angry parent, a new car driven carelessly and crashed!

"From now on, Ivor, you're on your own. You'll quit Orchard Acres, clear out and find a job and prove you can stick to it for a couple of years without one dime's help from me or from your grandfather. Understand? That way maybe you'll start to grow up a bit. As you are you're no use to Halliday Apples, not even as an office boy."

It was then that Ivor felt he'd taken more than enough. He had wrenched at his necklet till the ring broke and the gold maple leaf — emblem of Canada, which Ivor had worn since his schooldays — tinkled to the ground.

"If I'm as useless as you say, then better throw that in the bucket, Dad!"

Young Ivor had been shocked out of his crazy way of life. Shocked enough to flee from Ontario, make his way to India where he found work in a community hit by famine.

After that he found a job in Switzerland caring for homeless European children in a mountain village. It was there he heard of similar work in Scotland, in Knox House. Ivor Halliday had put his heart and his strength into all three jobs, just as Ruth had guessed, for his keep and a little pocket money.

So, what would he have to offer a wife? In his letter to his father Ivor had spoken about Ruth, the girl he had fallen in love with, the girl he wanted to spend the rest of his life with.

But even if Ruth did accept a proposal, what would they live on? Ivor knew he was as strong as an ox. Maybe he could make his way north, to the oil country, and earn enough money for two.

Santa's Special Gift

THE Market Inn party for the young carol-singers was a rip-roaring success. There was a sparkling Christmas tree, cakes and ice-cream, and a Santa Claus in a long red coat and with bushy beard and eyebrows.

No ordinary Santa Claus: this one was a magician as well, who brought white mice out of a hat, and plucked lollipops and balloons and small toys out of the air to throw to the laughing children.

Wee Hughie Bruce sat on the floor between his brothers. Hughie didn't like crowds, he never felt safe in a crowd, so at first he held on to Kit's jersey. And later when Santa Claus picked Kit to help with a magic trick, wee Hughie insisted on going,too. But the old man with the white whiskers and red coat just nodded and smiled, and his blue eyes twinkled like the stars on the tree.

By the time the party was over and the children were saying thank you to Mr and Mrs Ramsay, Hughie was feeling quite happy. Nobody had fussed him, or minded that he hardly spoke and kept so close to his brothers. Nobody had tried to separate them even in the games.

As Mrs Ramsay helped him on with his warm coat, Santa bent to speak to the little boy.

"Was it a good party, Hughie?"

And to Hughie's own surprise he heard himself speak quite loudly.

"It was awfu', awfu' good!"

Santa knelt and put his arms round Hughie and whispered in his ear.

"Do you think you could do something for me, Hughie?"

"What?" Hughie frowned.

"I want you to take a Chirstmas gift to someone."

"Who?" Kit and Willie Bruce were listening, very curious.

"I'll whisper, Hughie. This is to be a secret between you and me, right?" And the old gentleman whispered again into the little boy's ear. And wee Hughie smiled and nodded, and felt ten feet tall.

Santa Claus pressed a small package into his hand and closed his fingers tightly over it. Then he turned to Kit and Willie Bruce.

"This is Hughie's secret, now. No peeping, or questioning, please. OK, lads?" And the mystified pair promised.

LATER, Ruth was supervising the boys' nightly bath.

"Hughie, how can I wash you if you insist in not opening your hand?" she demanded.

For answer Hughie Bruce lifted one arm high above the water, his wee fist clenched tightly.

"He's awfu' scared you take it from him," Willie explained.

And Kit added, "It's a sort of secret between him and Santa Claus."

Ruth had had a very busy day. The last thing she wanted was a row with the children. And so she let wee Hughie have his way. She helped the boys to hang their Santa-bags at the foot of their beds, and she stayed with them till Hughie's eyes just wouldn't keep open any longer.

But, downstairs in the empty sitting-room, Ruth felt strangely flat that Christmas Eve and she knew that her low spirits had something to do with Ivor Halliday.

Ivor had been avoiding her all day. He had been really upset that no letter had come for him. He had shut the door of his cottage and only appeared for a silent lunch.

Ruth tried to keep herself busy, tidying up, and making last-minute preparations for the Christmas Day lunch. But she couldn't stop thinking that next Christmas there wouldn't be any nice cosy kitchen here, Knox House would be no more, the lovely garden a wilderness.

She hated the thought, too, that the three little Bruce brothers must go out of her life. What was in store for Kit and Willie and wee Hughie? After New Year would she ever see them again?

MIDNIGHT struck. Ruth crept up to the boys' room and carefully lifted the three Santa-bags and carried them downstairs. There were toys and sweets for each child — the kindly board of governors made sure of that. She crept upstairs with the loaded bags and fixed them in place.

As she came down again she heard a muffled knocking at the back door. Her heart leaped. It must be Ivor. At this late hour who else could it be?

It was Ivor!

"I guess I've a nerve calling so late. But I saw the light still on and I wanted to get rid of all this." He had an armful of wooden toys and he spilled them now on to the table. "Something for the kids, Ruth."

Ruth didn't even try to hide her feelings. She was overjoyed to see big Ivor, and glad, glad that he obviously thought so much about the children. He had willingly given up many spare hours making toys for them. She couldn't stop herself from hugging him.

And Ivor took full advantage of the hug. He pulled her closer and wouldn't let her go . . . not that Ruth Lyle tried very hard to get away. Ivor kissed her, and her answer was to snuggle the tip of her little nose into his ear.

Ivor's arms still held her a happy prisoner after their kisses ended.

"Ruth, listen, I've been doing some thinking. Now that we both have to leave here it's really hit me how much, how very, very much, I love you. I just can't imagine what my life would be like without you. I won't, *mustn't,* lose you.

"The sad thing is, my love," he went on, "I have nothing to offer you. Plainly my father has written me off. So I've only these." He held out his weather-brown hands. "And this . . ." And he thumped his forehead.

"My hands and my brains, Ruth. Could you marry a guy who has only hands and brains to offer?"

But still he wouldn't wait for her answer. Instead he kissed her again. Ruth's flower-blue eyes were wet with tears, but her lips gave him his answer.

They sat by the fire, talking. Ivor talked of his childhood in Orchard Acres, Ruth about London until Ivor suddenly tensed, listening.

"What's that?" Now Ruth heard, too. It was the sound of someone coming downstairs.

Santa's Special Gift

They watched and saw the kitchen door open very, very cautiously. There was a long pause and then a small sleep-tousled head appeared, round eyes staring.

"Hughie! Hughie Bruce, what are you doing out of your bed at this time!"

"Is it no' Christmas Day yet, Ruth?"

"This is the night Santa comes, Hughie, you ought to be asleep."

"He's been! My Santa-bag's all lumpy," Hughie said.

"There's to be no looking till daylight, Hughie. That wouldn't be fair to Kit and Willie."

"I didn' look, I just felt. I've got something for Ivor." Hughie opened his wee clenched fist and revealed a small package wrapped in white paper. Big Ivor took it.

"It's no' from me, Ivor, it's from Santa. The Santa at the carol party last night. The new Santa that did the magic tricks."

It struck Ruth that wee Hughie had not been heard to say so much for a long, long time. She went now to make him a warm milky drink.

She was putting the pan on the cooker when she heard Ivor Halliday cry out. It was a strange cry, the sound of sudden shock.

"What is it, Ivor?" she cried, turning back anxiously.

On Ivor's palm lay a shining gold maple leaf. The paper which had wrapped it round, was a letter.

Got your Christmas letter, Ivor. I couldn't wait any longer, I flew in a couple of days ago. Can't wait to see you, son; can't wait to have you home again. Remember I grabbed the maple leaf, Ivor? Well, I kept it, and here it is, and I'm proud to give it back. I'm booked in to the Market Inn over Christmas. I'll be along Christmas Day. And, by the way, I've been talking with your minister, Rev. Munn; he's put me in the picture about the kind of work you've been doing here among the children, and how the home is closing. He told me about the three small brothers who still haven't found a family. I thought of Orchard Acres and that great half-empty house and all the space in the world . . . Rev. Munn says it will take time, Ivor, all the legal raz-ma-taz and so forth, but he's sure he can work it. What a home we can give them at Orchard Acres; let's say it will be my way of saying "thank you, God" for a good son returned.

P.S. Ivor, I want to meet this Ruth. I'm sure she's a honey!

Heads close together, Ivor and Ruth read and re-read the wonderful letter. Wee Hughie Bruce cuddled in to Ivor's warm arms, but his round blue eyes were fixed on Ruth.

"What for are you crying, Ruth, what for?" he asked.

Ruth drew in a long, steadying breath.

"People sometimes cry because they're happy Hughie. And *I'm* happy."

"Me, too, Hughie," Ivor said. And he fixed the shining gold maple leaf back on the twisted ring of his necklet. □

Printed and Published in Great Britain by D. C. Thomson & Co. Ltd., Dundee, Glasgow, London and Manchester.
© D. C. Thomson & Co. Ltd., 1982.
ISBN 0 85116 264 9